denim revolution

Fashion is in the sky,
in the street;
fashion has to do with ideas,
the way we live,
what is happening.

—Coco Chanel

denim revolution

DOZENS OF WAYS TO TURN DENIM CAST-OFFS
INTO FASHION MUST-HAVES

NANCY MINSKY

POTTER
CRAFT

NEW YORK

Published in the United States by Potter Craft, an
imprint of the Crown Publishing Group, a division of
Random House, Inc., New York.
www.clarksonpotter.com
wwww.pottercraft.com

POTTER CRAFT and colophon is a registered trademark
of Random House, Inc.

Library of Congress Cataloging-in-Publication Data is
available upon request.

Printed in China

Design by Lauren Monchik
Photography by Alain Daussin and Michel Glik
Illustrations by Nancy Minsky

10 9 8 7 6 5 4 3 2 1

First Edition

contents

introduction

It's time for twenty-first-century dressmaking! And you're on the forefront of cool by being part of this evolution revolution, adapting dressmaking to our globally shared values and to fashion's delicious whims. This revolution is about enjoying and appreciating the beauty of recycling old into glamorous new, within the realities of our budgets, abilities, and free time. Denim is the universal numero uno fashion statement because it's so adaptable, no matter how diverse our lifestyles may be from continent to continent. It transcends political barriers, fills our pop culture, and clothes fashion stars, hippies, and rebels. By reinventing them—recycling jeans into new looks—we are making individual choices and creating a fab twenty-first century statement about personal style and freedom.

Whether you are a no-experience, all-thumbs type or a craft-nik who made her own wedding dress, if you love fashion and love denim, you can succeed with Denim Revolution (DR) projects. With your own two hands, you will lovingly and stylishly mix together old, new, vintage, antique, modern, and rugged in hip ways, to spice up your wardrobe without that designer price tag. Some of the projects take no previous experience and others require skillful craftsmanship. Whatever your level, just stick with me. I will guide you step-by-step, giving you the know-how to choose the projects that are right for you and the tools to adapt the designs to different body shapes and the variety of materials we will be using. Stand up to the suffocating stream of banality, the endless sales, and the piles of commercial clothes. Express your uniqueness and make your own individual statement!

Intrinsically cool denim is the perfect canvas to dress up, to re-accessorize, to reinvent. You will use lots of different needlecrafts, which offer a heartwarming relief from the high-tech, automated world that surrounds us. Embrace them, experiment, release your passion—you will reap the satisfying feeling of accomplishment and catch the designer bug.

Denim Revolution is divided into three sections. The first section lays the foundation. This is where you get started, with some basic denim background and useful tips and techniques. Please read it all! Then you move into the projects, which are laid out in five chapters—trashed-denim fashions followed by winter, spring, summer, and party clothes. Whatever your look—rocker, sporty, flirty, or sweet—

you'll find it here. Finally, in the back you can refer-
ence some basic DR know-how: ways to paint,
destroy, and reconstruct your denim.

My hope is that you take pleasure in the whole
creative process. Enjoy creating your wish list,
dreaming about the projects you will make, and
gathering the materials—bask in the pride of craftsmanship and the ability to say in response to compli-
ments, "Oh, thank you! I designed it and I made it!"

Remember, it's your party. Wear your new
wardrobe like a star designer! We've styled the photos with lots of ideas for wearing your projects, and
along with my fashion sketches, we hope they
inspire you to flaunt your handiwork. I am already
your biggest fan and supporter and would love to
see images of what you make. Be in touch via my
website, www.21centurydressmakers.com.

Bon courage,

Nancy

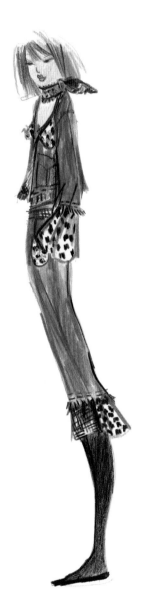

all about denim

To be a pro denim designer you need to fully appreciate denim's unique characteristics, so let's start with a little background. Denim is traditionally woven in 100 percent cotton yarn in a twill weave. The longer, stronger yarn runs parallel to the selvage (that is, the yarn runs the length of the fabric), and it is dyed indigo, a deep blue coloring originally derived from the indigo plant. The softer, shorter-spun yarn is cream-colored and runs perpendicularly to the indigo yarn. Today we see more and more variations on the basic cloth. For example, an ochre color may replace the cream, Lycra may be spun into the yarn to add stretch, and all kinds of washing effects may be applied to the finished garment to achieve special textures.

Denim has many different lives, from dark indigo to pale, soft, and worn. Look at your denim. There is a difference between the face and the wrong side of the material. It can be a subtle difference, but using the wrong side will add another texture to your designs. Notice and feel the different denim qualities, read the content labels, feel the different weights, and check out what happens when you cut, wash, and dry the denim. We all know that the indigo color fades with wear and washing, and the material softens, shreds, and frays in appealing and lovely ways. Observation and trial and error will help you gain control over your designs. Don't worry too much, though: Mistakes are often wonderful surprises, and denim is very forgiving.

Denim's signature details show off the tough nature of denim clothing, which is what gives DR designs their chic quality. The qualities found in jeans of all price ranges and from all decades are the fabulous, essential icing on the cake. The heavy finished seams, the rivets tacking the pockets, and the wear-and-tear on the knees and seams—these are what count when working with denim. These trims and details are so essential that this book has only one rule—one no-go—NO denim fabric by the yard allowed! The only denim used in this book comes from recycled clothing. Nothing beats the effects of converting an old pair of jeans into something else, and they can't be achieved if you cut from fabric by the yard. So start thinking about the various denim characteristics and experiment, explore, cut, wash, appliqué, and play. You'll soon be taking denim into the twenty-first century.

getting started

Start by browsing through the book, so you will have an overall sense of what DR is all about. Taste the variety of projects, crafts, and the different skill levels. Then zero in on your personal style and comfort zone. The user-friendly instructions speak to you directly and answer your questions. They are organized into the following sections:

Your Challenge

This is your design challenge. As a designer, you need to imagine what, why, and how to make something that you would desperately love to have in your wardrobe. Your challenge is to make it happen. Let your imagination roam and your energy and determination surge when you read the descriptive challenge. Then it's your call—are you going to take the challenge?

How Difficult

The levels of difficulty are labeled Beginner, Easy, Intermediate, and Experienced. If you are new to the craft, start with an easier level, build up your skill and your confidence, and then move to a harder one. The level of difficulty is based on how long it takes to complete the project and how much prior experience is needed. Still, this varies by individual—one person will know how to sew, another is not a sewer but knows how to stencil—so what may be very easy for you may be difficult for someone else. Also, one person may be looking for a weekend project, while another needs an immediate fashion fix. What I describe here are the skills and time needed to complete the project so you can best choose what works for you time-, craft-, and

skill-wise. All the projects are very chic, regardless of how difficult they are.

What Denim Do I Need?

Choosing the right denim is key, since it's the base for your project. You will recycle denim from your own wardrobe or gather discards from friends, family, garage sales, or wherever you find interesting, disused denim. Since it's all recycled, I assume that each of us may use different denim for a project. Read my descriptions and the characteristics I looked for in my denim to help you choose your denim and adapt the instructions for your purposes. All the photos, patterns, and instructions are in adult size Medium. Take time to read my comments on how to make necessary adjustments to fit your body and style.

What Other Materials Will I Need?

When "Sewing Basket" is listed, it refers to your stash of basic sewing tools that should include:

- 3 pairs of scissors! Cutting denim takes muscle, and good scissors are the essential tool that you can't skimp on. You will need a pair of long cutting shears with about 8" (20cm) blades, medium-sized ones with 5"–6" (12–15cm) blades, and a pair of small embroidery scissors
- Assortment of hand-sewing needles, including needles for general sewing, heavy-duty needles for denim and leather, and fine needles for beads
- Box of straight pins
- Pin cushion
- Seam ripper
- Thimble
- Spools of thread in assorted colors for basting
- Tailor's chalk
- Tape measure
- Yardstick
- Ruler

The other materials listed in this section are the special ones needed for that particular project. Read my descriptions and study the photos. The materials you use are an important element in achieving the designer's touch. Wonderful trims for embellishing your projects are available in a wide selection from the Internet, garage sales, attics, flea markets, neighborhood sewing shops, home furnishing shops, craft shops, and hardware stores. The search is part of the fun of design. What you find will determine your personal slant on the project, and browsing all the sources is stimulating and eye-opening. I have listed all the details of the trims I've used to serve as a guide when you assemble your own embellishments. Improvise with wonderful recycled "finds" from your closet or copy what I used.

How to Do It Step by Step

Here are your instructions, the tips and visuals that will guide you to success. Before you start a project, read through and study this material to get a clear overall understanding of what you are going to do. That way, you'll also get a sense of the order of the steps and reasons behind them. You should feel comfortable with the project before you even begin.

insider scoop: tips and techniques for successful designs

I have a big cardboard box—I call it my "I-Box" (Idea Box)—into which I toss all my denim scraps. Do it! You will be amazed how often you find yourself digging through the box and finding things you thought were worthless but are now defining your look!

If you get frustrated or feel suddenly lost, don't fret. This is part of the creative process. It's good, not bad! It's proof that you are challenging yourself. So stop, step away from your project, have a cup of tea or a day off, whatever you need to reenergize and give yourself some space. When you pick it up again, you will have fresh eyes and will see clearly what to do. Sometimes this means ripping out something that did not go well, or even stopping that project and starting another one. The key is to keep going; you will work your

way out of the dumps and into brand-new territory.

Some of the patterns will need to be adjusted to your size. To do this, cut the patterns in the middle, horizontally, and vertically. At the cutting lines, either enlarge the patterns by adding strips of paper, or reduce them by overlapping and taping the joins to make them smaller. Then with a pencil, reshape the new outer line smoothly. *Voilà!* This is basic pattern making—grading the patterns to fit you—and you can do it!

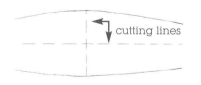

cutting lines

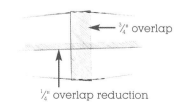

¾" overlap

¼" overlap reduction

Often I say to cut the fabric on the bias or on the diagonal. This is because even sturdy denim will relax and drape more softly when used on the bias. The bias is the true diagonal from the length or selvage. To find the bias on your jeans, assume that the length of the material is running down the center of the pant leg front and back. True bias will be at a 45 degree angle from the center line of the pants.

Gather all the materials for the project before you start! There are many different kinds of embroidery floss, but for DR, we only need thick, colorful thread, and any variety will work. I generally use 6-strand DMC embroidery floss because it comes in small quantities, and I like to have a choice of colors on hand. But on some projects, I used other types of embroidery floss because they were in my sewing box and the colors were beautiful.

When cutting fur, first draw the cutting line on the wrong side with tailor's chalk. Then cut on your line using either small scissors, an X-acto knife, or a one-sided razor blade. Carefully cut only the backing and not the hairs.

If you will be adding other fabrics or ribbons to your denim, you will need to decide how you will clean the garment. If you intend to hand or machine wash it, create a test swatch. Appliqué your fabrics and trims on a similar scrap of denim. Depending on how you intend to care for the garment, machine wash and dry it or hand wash and line dry, then press it. Now how does it look? Did the fabric shrink or fade? Unexpected results are sometimes wonderful. The deciding factor is whether you like the look.

Be comfortable when you work. You need good lighting and a comfortable chair. Sit with good posture. If you are cutting, use a cutting table or a high countertop to keep from bending at an awkward angle.

Take time to press or machine wash and dry swatches as needed along the way.

Securely knot and hide all sewing thread ends, so they won't unravel, be seen, or be felt.

Edge finishes are an important style element, even when they look natural and haphazard. Denim can be left with raw frayed edges or machine zigzag stitched, embroidered, and so on. It depends on whether you want the edge light and airy or structured and stiff—whether you want contrasting thread or matching. These are very important DR decisions, so make test swatches, check the look, and then apply the treatment to the actual project.

When you search for your trims for the projects, keep your focus on the descriptions in the challenge and the overall effect you want to achieve.

Before you cut, paint, or permanently alter your denim, do a test! Pin a skirt hem and try it on to check the length, for example. Getting the proportions just right requires a little bit of experimentation and give and take. And remember, all views are important—front, side, and back. So make sure you are getting the look you're going for by checking all views in a full-length mirror.

Sometimes I ask you to use silk thread. Please do, as its pretty luster really changes a project's look. You'll appreciate the thread's beauty when you wear the denim. Metallic threads and lots of novelty colors are also available, so experiment with different accents the way a designer would. This is how you define your denim style, your signature look.

When you slash your fabric horizontally, you will see mainly a blue frayed edge; vertically slashing reveals white, and slashing on the bias produces a plusher, fuller blue-and-white frayed edge.

hot denim blues

Let it rip! Deconstructed clothes know no limits—this chapter is for raw and reckless

eco-revelers and snowboard freaks. Beginners and experienced designers, express yourself.

YOUR CHALLENGE

Do you have a beautiful hand-me-down sweater, something lovingly and carefully hand knit that now has moth holes and wear-and-tear? Resurrect it with class, British aristocratic know-how, and style! Stitch on oversized, rugged denim elbow patches and make those moth holes hot!

Transform a pair of basic indigo jeans into ones that have lived a life on the hip side of the tracks. This is your chance to use all those designer techniques you love or want to try—bleach, rip, cut, sand, stitch, paint, or patch. Do the jeans look masculine or feminine? Doesn't matter! It's just too cool and too fun!

**moth holes bite the dust sweater
and denim destroy jeans**

moth holes bite the dust sweater and denim destroy jeans

How Difficult?

Beginner. Takes half an hour.

What Denim Do I Need?

Denim scraps for elbow patches. I used a stone-washed dark indigo shade, 100 percent cotton.

What Other Materials Will I Need?

Your "Sewing Basket" (page 11)

Photocopy of Elbow Patch pattern (page 118)

Vintage wool sweater

Deep red embroidery floss

My project is made with a real family heirloom, one of my mom's handknit creations. My mom happens to be an extraordinarily gifted knitter and taught me, and everyone else who dropped by, to knit.

Don't throw away your favorite old sweaters just because moths have made a meal of them or ladders are running up and down it. There are plenty of chic ways to cut, sew, and recycle these wonderful old knits.

moth holes bite the dust sweater

HOW TO DO IT STEP BY STEP

1. **Make Elbow Patches:** Using the Elbow Patch pattern on page 118, cut 2 denim elbow patches. Machine wash, dry, and press.

2. **Sew Patches:** Pin the patches on the elbows of the sweater and baste. Remove the pins and hand-sew in a running stitch with the red thread about ¼" (6mm) from the denim edge.

Make it a work in progress—add denim patches as new holes appear in the sweater or when you find interesting denim bits.

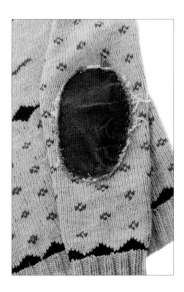

How Difficult?

Easy. This project takes no experience, because anything and everything you do is okay. But it takes time, muscle, and determination, as you must work on it for quite a few hours to make it interesting.

What Denim Do I Need?

A pair of dark indigo jeans that fit the way you like jeans to fit, whether loose or tight. I used a pair of Levi's 501, size 31W 30L and a variety of faded denim scraps to appliqué.

What Other Materials Will I Need?

Your "Sewing Basket" (page 11)

Sewing machine

Ochre and denim thread

Red, yellow, and black fabric paint

White and bronze fabric spray paint

Red permanent fabric marker

Bleach

Coarse sandpaper

½ yard (45cm) of 1" (2.5cm) wide red woven cotton braid

denim destroy jeans

HOW TO DO IT STEP BY STEP

1. **Stress Your Jeans:** Just go for it! Here is the list of everything I did to those jeans: I slashed short and long holes diagonally, horizontally, and vertically. Around some of the holes I pulled threads to achieve the super-worn look. I patched one of the slashes from behind, and then zigzag machine stitched back and forth all over the patch with denim thread. I scribbled words with permanent markers, spray painted and splashed paint like Jackson Pollack. I bleached and sanded. Look at Paint Stuff (page 114) and Add Wear-and-Tear to Your Jeans (page 115) for more ideas or techniques.

2. **Sew on Red Braid:** Highlight your cuff turn-back with some bright braid. Cut the braid in half. Starting at the cuff, pin one half to the side seam overlapping the inside seam allowance. Trim to fit. Baste, remove pins, and machine sew around the perimeter of the braid. Repeat on remaining cuff.

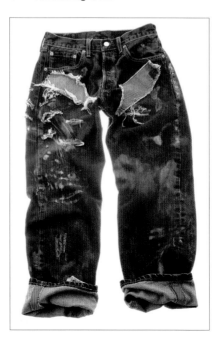

skater dude nu-wave cap

YOUR CHALLENGE

It's time to cover an old baseball cap with signature denim bits that you love. You will pin, cut, sew, remove the visor, spray paint, stencil, and do a bit of all the crafts in this book to make a one-of-a- kind cap. Hats are wonderful, the symbols of confident cool, so do your thing, let your designer juices flow naturally, and make it fabulous!

skater dude nu-wave cap

How Difficult?

Easy. This cap takes no skill, only desire. Yes, you are going to use a seam ripper, paint, and sew, but this can even be a first-time project because whatever mess you make, it will still be perfectly cool! It takes about an hour depending on how much you gussy it up. I used the sewing machine, but you could also hand-sew this project.

What Denim Do I Need?

You need a bunch of denim scraps, with seams, tack buttons, belt loops, and even stenciled scraps. Gather together an assortment of different denim textures because when you're designing you need choices to play with. If you add a new D-ring cinch like I did, you also need two 5" x 1" (12.5cm x 2.5cm) denim strips.

What Other Materials Will I Need?

Your "Sewing Basket" (page 11)

A baseball cap, dig through your closet, and recycle one

2 D-rings, 1" (2.5cm) diameter

Sewing machine

Ochre thread

Masking tape

White and copper fabric spray paint

Newspaper

HOW TO DO IT STEP BY STEP

1. **Remove the Visor:** First, you need to get rid of the visor so you have just a skull cap. The best way to do this is to open the seam with a seam ripper, remove the visor, and then re-stitch the seam closed with ochre thread on the sewing machine.

2. **Change the Back Cinch:** The back Velcro cinch on my cap was stiff and too perfect so I removed it with a seam ripper. Then I replaced it with the denim strips and D-ring as follows. Slide the D-rings through one strip. Fold the strip in half and pin it to the left side of the cap. The position is the same as the original cinch. Baste in place and remove the pins. Machine stitch ¼" (6mm) all around the edge of the strip, where it joins the cap, as close as you can sew to the D-rings. Pin the other strip to the right side, again in the same position as the original cinch. Machine stitch ¼" (6mm) all around the edge of the strip where it joins the cap. See **diagram 1**.

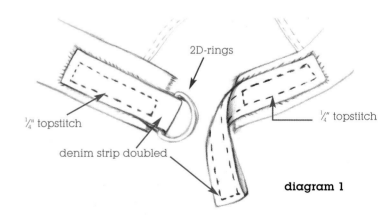

2D-rings

$\frac{1}{4}$" topstitch

$\frac{1}{4}$" topstitch

denim strip doubled

diagram 1

3. **Decorate Your Cap:** Pin the various denim scraps you gathered on your cap. When you like the way it looks, try it on, adjust if necessary, and then baste the patches in place. Remove the pins. Machine sew with ochre thread ⅜" (9mm) from the raw edge, all around each patch. Check out the photos of what I did for inspiration.

4. **Add a Stencil:** To make a "gurl" stencil, print the word on paper using your computer. The word I used in this project was in Century Gothic, size 175, set bold, outline. Cut out the letters carefully. Then cut the paper to a more manageable shape, cutting the border around "gurl" to about 1½" (3.8cm). Lay newspaper down to protect the workspace. Tape the stencil as flat as possible on the cap and spray paint over it. When it's dry, remove the stencil.

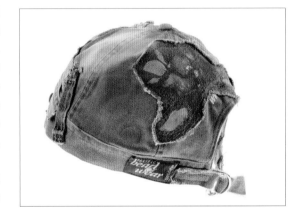

5. **When you finish,** spray paint your cap here and there with a few swishes to add texture. You can also slash or rip it. Do your own thing, have fun, let it evolve. Check out Paint Stuff (page 114) and Add Wear-and-Tear to Your Jeans (page 115) for more ideas.

YOUR CHALLENGE

Let loose and create a wildly ripped, wonderful new pair of cool shorts. You will cut and slash and cut and slash. It's all about scissors with a few swishes of spray paint and a few hand stitches. I want to see pocket linings and flesh showing. It's time to release all your stress and angst and recycle in a big way.

time out! cargo shorts

time out! cargo shorts

How Difficult?

Beginner. Takes no experience—just desire and passion. But be patient. To do it up right, it does take time—a couple of hours to dismantle and reshape your jeans. The only sewing is about 8 hand stitches.

What Denim Do I Need?

I used a pair of oversized men's cargo pants, 100 percent lightweight cotton in a dark, slightly stonewashed shade of denim. They were stamped "Sample" and bought in a secondhand clothing store. The fit should be baggy, and the funkier the pockets the better.

What Other Materials Will I Need?

Your "Sewing Basket" (page 11)

2 copper D-rings, 1½" (3.8cm) diameter

Denim blue embroidery floss

White fabric spray paint

Newspaper

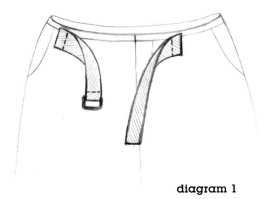

diagram 1

HOW TO DO IT STEP BY STEP

1. **Cut the Shorts and Cuffs:** Cut the cuffs off the jeans, 1½" (3.8cm) from the bottom. (These cuffs will become your new waist cincher in Step 2.) Cut the waistband off ½" (13mm) above its lower sewing line so the shorts will hang a bit looser. Finally, cut the pant length to measure 22" (56cm) long from the natural waistline. A 22" (56cm) pant length is knee length on me, size Medium. But before you cut your jeans, try them on, and decide on the length that's best for you—knee, calf, ankle. It's your DR call.

2. **Make the Waist Cinch:** Add a front waist cinch. The 2 strips cut from the cuffs, should measure about 1½" x 9" (3.8cm x 23cm) long. Slide one denim strip through the 2 D-rings, fold the strip in half, and pin the cut edges to the right waistband, about 1½" (3.8cm) from the pocket edge as shown in **diagram 1**. With the embroidery floss, attach the two cut edges securely to the pants with a few backstitches. Then hand sew a row of backstitches ½" (13mm) from the fold, so the D-rings will stay in place. Pin the other strip to the left waistband, about 3" (7.5cm) from the front edge, and backstitch securely 1" (2.5cm) from the belt edge.

3. **Slash the Jeans:** Totally cut up your jeans with lots of different textures: long slashes, little pricks, small cuts—horizontally, vertically, and diagonally. Then machine wash and dry. Try them on and see how they look. Need more slashing? Do it! Want more skin exposed? Cut some more! When you try the jeans on, mark with tailor's chalk the areas that need more slashing.

4. **Add Some Spray Paint:** Protect your work area with newspaper. Lay the jeans on the newspaper, front side up. Spray paint swishes to emphasize the wear and tear. As you work, step back, check the look, and then spray more as needed. When it's dry, about 5 or 10 minutes, repeat on the back and then on the left and right sides.

enchanted blues

This chapter is about clothes and accessories created for downtown rendezvous and uptown dinner dates. It's about savvy, chic city wear: delightful contrasts in attitude, surprising combinations of patterns, and daring ways to express your individuality and designer talents!

YOUR CHALLENGE

Create an upscale, new-look skirt. It's got to be very stylish and special, with a pleated hem done up with interesting detailing. The luxe fabrics give the skirt a stunning swing when you walk. You will cut, sew, pin, match plaids, and add designer detailing. If, like me, you want it to match Downtown Babe on page 50. then create a new-suit look, checking that your denims blend and trims match. Whichever way you go, I suggest you use the finest materials you can find and afford to get a unique luxe-rugged look.

flip skirt

flip skirt

How Difficult?

Intermediate. Matching the checks and pleating them evenly takes some patience and experience, and that attention to detail is key to this high-fashion look. If you are short on experience, use a fabric without a geometric pattern—instead of the plaids use florals, paisleys, or solids—so that imperfections in the handwork are hidden instead of being amplified by the bold checks. The project takes a day to complete.

What Denim Do I Need?

The key here is the fit. You want a skirt that hugs your bum—or fits the way you like. I used a slim fitted skirt, H&M L.O.G.G. in 100 percent cotton, with a washed look. Once I took out the hem, my skirt measured 19½" (49.5cm) from the bottom of the waistband to the bottom of the hem. The width at the hem is 19" (48.5cm). Compare the pocket and skirt details on your skirt to the photos to be certain that your skirt will adapt to the design.

What Other Materials Will I Need?

Your "Sewing Basket" (page 11)

½ yard (0.5m) cream and black houndstooth check woolen fabric

Sewing machine

Cream sewing thread

½ yard (0.5m) glen plaid worsted wool fabric

Burgundy embroidery floss

Photocopy of Pocket Flap pattern (page 121)

12" x 12" (30.5cm x 30.5cm) square of floral-print silk charmeuse

10 black and silver assorted gorgeous buttons, approximately ½" (13mm)–¾" (2cm) in diameter

HOW TO DO IT STEP BY STEP

1. **Decide on the Skirt Length:** Choose the final skirt length you want. Let out the hem to add length (as I did), or cut the skirt shorter if you want less length. Keep in mind that your finished skirt length will be 3½" (9cm) longer than the original skirt.

What does your bottom hem opening measure? If it measures more or less than my project (19" (48.5cm)), then the 24" (61cm) glen plaid strips may need to be longer or shorter as well. So before you cut your material, measure your skirt, read through all the instructions, and check out the diagrams.

2. **Cut the Houndstooth:** Cut a 6" x 24" (15cm x 61cm) strip from the houndstooth check. With cream thread, machine zigzag stitch all around the edge. Press using a pressing cloth.

3. **Make the Houndstooth Hem:** Following **diagram 1,** form a 2" (5cm) deep box pleat at the center of the houndstooth. Align the box pleat at the center back of the skirt with the denim overlapping the houndstooth by 1" (2.5cm). Pin a 1½" (3.8cm) deep pleat on either side of the box pleat, spaced 2¼" (5.5cm) from the center back. Baste and remove the pins.

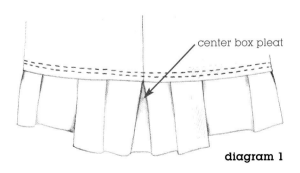

center box pleat

diagram 1

If you are using plaids or a fabric with a pattern, adapt the pleating measurements to fit the repeat in your plaid. My tuck measurements are based on the repeat in the glen plaid. This is designer know-how, and you can do it—just play with it a bit!

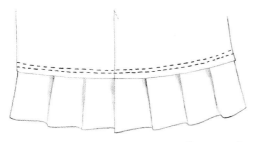

diagram 2

Before cutting the flaps, check their size. The flap should slip smoothly into the pocket. If necessary, enlarge or reduce the pattern to fit your skirt.

4. **Cut the Glen Plaid:** Cut two 4½" x 24" (11.5cm x 61cm) strips of the glen plaid check. With cream thread, machine zigzag stitch all around the edge. Press using a pressing cloth.

5. **Make the Glen Plaid Hem:** Following **diagram 2**, pin the plaid to the hem. My skirt has a front slit opening, so I began there, aligning the glen plaid at the front edge with a 1½" (3.8cm) fold under, then pleated the glen plaid every 2¾" (6.5cm), ¾" (2cm) deep. If your skirt doesn't have a front slit opening, the tucks should continue smoothly in front without any interruption. The denim hem should overlap the glen plaid by 1" (2.5cm). At the back, fold under the glen plaid 1½" (3.8cm). Pin, baste, and remove the pins. Using burgundy embroidery floss and following **diagrams 1** and **2**, stitch the plaid to the denim with two lines of running stitch, ⅜" (1cm) and ¾" (2cm) above the denim hem. Remove all basting.

6. **Make the Pocket Flaps:** Using the Pocket Flap pattern on page 121, cut out 2 houndstooth and 2 silk floral flaps, flipping the pattern so you have a left and right side.

With wrong sides together, pin 1 piece of silk to 1 piece of houndstooth. Baste and remove the pins. Gently machine zigzag stitch all around the edge. Because the flaps are cut on the bias, they are very elastic, so be careful not to stretch them out of shape as you sew. Remove the basting. Repeat with the other flap pieces. Gently press using a pressing cloth.

Tuck the flaps ¾" (2cm) into the pockets. Pin, baste, and remove the pins. Using burgundy embroidery floss, sew with a running stitch ½" (2cm) from the edge. Arrange 5 buttons charmingly on each flap. Sew the buttons on snugly, with a continuous thread, securely knotting after each button.

7. Trim the Waistband: Cut a strip of the glen plaid check fabric 1¾" (4.5cm) x the length of your waistband minus 5" (12.5cm). With cream thread, machine zigzag stitch all around the edge. Press with a pressing cloth. Pin it to the waistband with the center of the strip aligned with the center back waist and set ¼" (6mm) below the top of the waistband. Baste and remove pins. Using burgundy embroidery floss and following **diagram 3,** stitch two lines of running stitch, ¼" (6mm) and ¾" (2cm) below the top edge of the plaid.

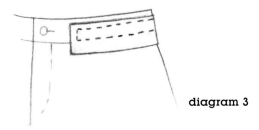

diagram 3

8. Final Finish: Press the denim hem carefully on the wrong side, with a pressing cloth. This is a fine designer garment, so treat it with care and dry clean only.

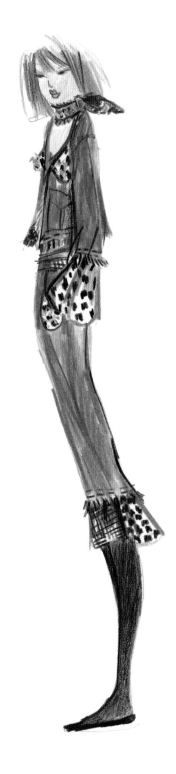

YOUR CHALLENGE

For this project you have your choice of two fabulously cool cuff bracelet designs. They are funky, high-fashion fun. One is gold chained and leopard spotted, while the other has hip patent leather cutouts. They're easy sewing projects. With a little stitching and cutting, you can put the pieces together like a puzzle. Your choice, one or a pair— it's a glam look!

leopard and patent leather cuffs

2-cool cuffs

How Difficult?

Easy. You only need to be able to do the simplest machine- and hand-sewing. Each cuff takes at most one hour to complete.

What Denim Do I Need?

Scraps—a couple of different shades of denim, all basic, sturdy, 100 percent cotton denim (it will hold the shape).

What Other Materials Will I Need?

Your "Sewing Basket" (page 11)

8" (20.5cm; or your cuff length) of 1" (2.5cm) wide Mokuba Suede Leopard ribbon, #4855

Sewing machine

Denim blue thread

8" (20.5cm; or your cuff length) x ⅜" (1cm) wide gold chain

Purple embroidery floss

2¼" x ¾" wide (5.5cm x 2cm) black iron-on Velcro

leopard cuff

HOW TO DO IT STEP BY STEP

1. **Cut the Denim:** Cut a scrap of denim to 3" x 8" (7.5cm x 20.5cm). Before cutting, hold the denim on your wrist to make sure it will fit with a ½" (13mm) overlap at the closure. If necessary, adjust size to fit. Cut another denim scrap the same length but 1" (2.5cm) wide. Machine wash and dry the denim strips to create soft, fringed edges. Press.

2. **Trim the Cuff:** Pin the spotted suede ribbon down the center of the wider strip of denim. Baste, remove the pins, and machine zigzag stitch around the 4 edges of the ribbon. Hand-sew the chain link securely and smoothly down the center of the ribbon with purple embroidery floss. Cut the 1" (2.5cm) denim strip in half lengthwise. Align the frayed edge of one strip with the edge of the suede ribbon. Pin, baste, remove the pins, and machine zigzag stitch on the cut edge. Repeat with the other strip on the other side of the ribbon. Remove the basting.

3. **Make the Closure:** Cut the Velcro down the length, so that it is only ⅜" (10mm) wide. Position the Velcro at the overlap and press in place.

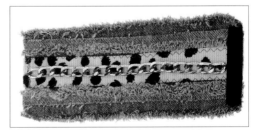

What Other Materials Will I Need?

Your "Sewing Basket"
(page 11)

Photocopy of Patent Leather Cuff pattern
(page 118)

4" x 9" (10cm x 23cm) patent leather (or the length of your cuff)

Sewing machine

Denim blue thread

2¼" x ¾" wide (5.5cm x 2cm) black iron-on Velcro

This is the only slightly tricky part of this project, because the denim and patent leather have different give. Take your time to keep the fabrics flat and well aligned.

patent leather cuff

HOW TO DO IT STEP BY STEP

1. **Cut the Denim:** Cut a scrap of denim to 3" x 8" (7.5cm x 20.5cm).

Before cutting, hold the denim on your wrist to make sure it will fit with a ½" (13mm) overlap at the closure. If necessary, adjust size to fit.

Cut out the triangle shapes from the Patent Leather Cuff pattern, pin the pattern to the denim cuff, and mark the triangles with tailor's chalk. Remove the pins and, using small scissors, cut each triangle out of the denim. Machine wash, dry, and press.

2. **Sew the Denim to the Patent Leather:** With the right side up, lay the denim on top of the right side of the patent leather and pin together. Baste, remove the pins, and machine zigzag stitch ¼" (6mm) from the edge all around the outer cuff edge. Remove the basting. Machine zigzag stitch around each triangle cutout, ⅛" (3mm) from the cut edge. Trim the patent leather around the outer edge to ⅛" (3mm) beyond the denim edge.

3. **Press the Cuff:** Using a pressing cloth, very gently press using a low heat setting on the wrong side to set the stitching lines.

4. **Make the Closure:** Cut the Velcro down the length, so that it is only ⅜" (10mm) wide. Position the Velcro at the overlap and press in place.

uptown chic ascots

YOUR CHALLENGE

Craft a stunning, chic ascot. The frayed denim edges contrasting with luxe silk are shaggy chic and all the rage. I've made three of them already, so be careful! Once you start, it's hard to put on the brakes! Relieve your itch to design, cut, pin, and sew to make a scarf in a flash of color and pattern of your choice.

lace ascot

How Difficult?

Easy. Takes an hour to make. There are three versions scattered throughout the photos. Retro and Butterfly are the same but use different silks; the Lace Variation has lace edging.

What Denim Do I Need?

Softly worn and washed pieces of cotton denim that will fit the Ascot pattern (page 118) twice on the bias

What Other Materials Will I Need?

Your "Sewing Basket" (page 11)

Sewing machine

Ecru silk thread

FOR THE RETRO AND BUTTERFLY VARIATIONS:

Printed silk that will fit the Ascot pattern on the bias

Photocopy of Ascot pattern (page 118)

Ochre thread plus thread in a color that blends with the ground color of your silk

FOR THE LACE VARIATION:

36" (91cm) of 1" (2.5cm) wide ecru cotton lace trim

36" (91cm) 1½" (3.8cm) wide) ecru cotton netting trim

36" (91cm) ½" (13mm) wide olive cotton ribbon

retro and butterfly variations

HOW TO DO IT STEP BY STEP

1. **Cut the Denim:** Cut 2 pieces of the denim using the ascot pattern on page 118. Overlap the 2 pieces ½" (13mm), at the back neck. Pin, baste, and remove pins. Sew down the middle of the overlap with ochre thread and zigzag stitch. Machine wash and dry. Press.

2. **Cut the Silk Print:** Cut two pieces of the silk on the bias from the Ascot pattern as you did for the denim.

3. **Attach the Silk to the Denim:** Lay the silk neatly on the denim, with the edges aligned and wrong sides together. The silk will overlap ½" (13mm) at the center back neck. Pin in place, baste, and remove the pins. With the silk fabric on top, and using ochre thread in the bobbin and the other color for the top spool, machine zigzag stitch all around the edges of the ascot, ¼" (6mm) from the edge. Stitch down the center back silk overlap.

4. **Final touches:** Neatly knot and hide loose ends of the threads. Press on the denim side.

lace variation

HOW TO DO IT STEP BY STEP:

1. **Cut the Denim:** Follow step 1 of the Retro and Butterfly Version.

2. **Cut the Silk:** Cut 2 pieces of the silk on the bias from the Ascot pattern on page 118.

3. **Trim the Silk:** Cut 16" (40.5cm) of each of the 3 trims. Sew the 3 ribbons together to form a wide border as follows. Pin the olive ribbon to the cotton netting trim, with the olive ribbon overlapping the cotton netting by ⅜" (1cm). Baste, remove pins. With the ecru silk thread, zigzag stitch along the edge of the olive ribbon. Repeat, pinning this piece to the lace trim, with the lace overlapping the netting by ⅜" (1cm). Baste, remove pins and zigzag stitch along the edge of the netting. Pin the wide border to the edge of one of the silk ascot pieces, with the silk overlapping the border by ½" (13mm). Add tucks to the lace, about ⅜" (1cm) deep, about every 1½" (3.8cm), so the lace follows the curved shape of the silk. Baste in place and remove the pins. Machine zigzag stitch the border to the silk with ecru thread down the center of the overlap. Remove all basting. Repeat for the other silk piece.

4. **Final touches:** Follow steps 3 and 4 of the Retro and Butterfly Version, on page 34.

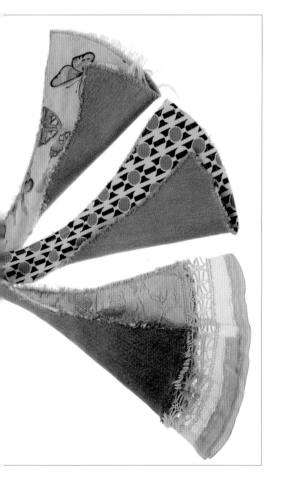

butterfly, retro, and lace ascots

YOUR CHALLENGE

Dress yourself in a pair of hip, underground-style jeans. The Cat's Meow features raw edges, lots of hand embroidery, and asymmetrical styling. You will sew cool leather pouches on the hips for your cell. For the dark color palette you will wrap black lace, leather, jet beads, and Spanish braid seductively around your body, and accent it with feminine blush velvet ribbons. It's a daredevil project with a knock-out attitude.

the cat's meow jeans

the cat's meow jeans

How Difficult?

Experienced. The Cat's Meow is a challenge, a labor of love. If you are a passionate hand-sewer and have some experience sewing different textures, this is your dream project. Look at the photos and then create your own version. The key to DR styling is the asymmetrical look, where one leg has a patch while the other has a racing stripe up the side. Keep your denim, lace, and trim colors dark, except for the pale blush accent. This is high-style designer fashion, requiring a few days of contemplation to get it just right.

What Denim Do I Need?

Jeans that fit slim with a narrow leg. I used Slim Fit Stretch jeans from the Gap, in a stonewashed, black-indigo shade.

What Other Materials Will I Need?

Your "Sewing Basket" (page 11)

12" x 12" (30.4cm x 30.4cm) piece of black leather

Photocopies of Pouch and Flap patterns (page 120)

Brown, purple, black, gray, and blush embroidery floss

¾" x 6" (2cm x 15cm) piece of iron-on black Velcro

½ (50cm) yard black polyester lace fabric

3 yards (3m) ½" (13mm) wide black curly Spanish braid

2 yards (2m) ⅝" (15mm) wide blush polyester crushed velvet ribbon

24" (61cm) 1¼" (3cm) wide jet-black beaded trim

Black thread

1 yard (1 m) ⅝" (15mm) wide burgundy velvet ribbon with picot edge

4" x 8" (10cm x 20.5cm) scrap of printed burgundy velvet

HOW TO DO IT STEP BY STEP

1. **Make the Pouches:** Using leather, cut out the Pouch and Flap patterns from leather.

Before cutting, check that the pattern fits your cell phone or whatever you want to stash in the pouch. Resize if necessary—this is customized DR!

Whipstitch around the perimeter of the pouches and the flaps with brown embroidery floss. Pin one pouch to your jeans on the right high hip area, as shown on page 39, forming ½" (13mm) tucks at the bottom corners of the pouch. Try the jeans on to make sure you like the positioning. Sew in place with brown embroidery floss, using a backstitch along the sides and bottom, ⅜" (1cm) from the edge. Align the pouch flap on top of the pouch. Pin in place. With backstitch, sew ⅝" (1.5cm) from the straight edge with brown embroidery floss. Cut a 2" (5cm) strip of Velcro, align the flap, and apply the Velcro. Repeat with the other pouch on the left high hip area.

Pin as little as necessary along the stitching line, as every pin poke will leave a mark on the leather.

The pouches are the most difficult part of the project. It's difficult to get your hands comfortably inside the jeans to sew them on—so persevere.

2. **Apply the Lace:** Cut out 3 pieces of lace to appliqué on the jeans. Use the photos for inspiration. I appliquéd a long piece to the front starting 1" (2.5cm) below the waistband and ending above the knee. It measures 5" (12.5cm) at the widest part and touches the pouch, drawing the two pieces together visually. Another lace piece overlaps the right back pocket in a leaf-like shape. The

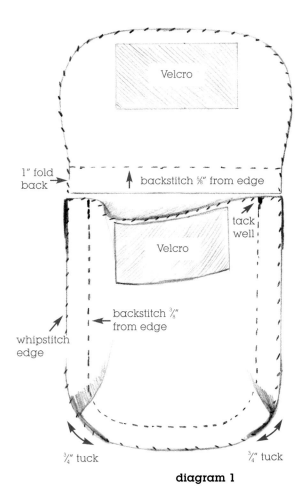

1" fold back

backstitch ⅝" from edge

Velcro

tack well

Velcro

whipstitch edge

backstitch ⅜" from edge

¾" tuck   ¾" tuck

diagram 1

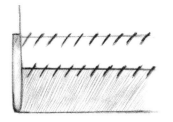

diagram 2

last is a jagged piece of lace crossing over the right side seam, drawing the two other lace shapes together. Use it as a guide, as you adapt to your body shape, jeans, and lace. Black lace is gorgeous on dark jeans and will look awesome in whatever shapes you cut. The trick is to sew it properly to your jeans. Loosely pin, leaving some slack to allow for the stretch in the jeans (not in the lace), and baste in place. Try the jeans on to see what happens on the body—adjust if the lace doesn't have enough slack. Once you are satisfied with the placement, baste, remove pins, and whipstitch with embroidery stitch all around the lace edges. Remove the basting. I used gray thread and when I finished the skein, I used purple thread. Using different colors created interest, but just so you get the idea—it's an individual free flowing project depending on what you have in your sewing box or your favorite colors!

3. Stitch on the Spanish Braid: Using the photos for inspiration, pin the black Spanish braid in place in a swirly fashion. Start at the right front pocket, swirl around the lace appliqués and end at the back waist. Baste, remove pins and whipstitch with embroidery floss. As with the lace, I alternated embroidery colors, using black thread, switching to brown and then purple.

4. Jazz Up the Cuffs: With a seam ripper, open the side seam 5" (12.5cm) from the cuff. Cut the cuff off ¼" (6mm) above the hem-stitching line and open the hem with a seam ripper. Following **diagram 2**, sandwich the cuff into the folded hem. Pin, baste, remove the pins, and whipstitch the cuff in place with black embroidery floss, as shown in **diagram 2.**

5. Stitch on the Blush Velvet Ribbon: Pin the ribbon in the cuff slit opening. Baste, remove the pins, and, with the blush embroidery floss, stitch in place with a simple running stitch all around the perimeter of the ribbon. Remove the basting. Sew the ribbon to the waistband with the same steps. The ribbon wraps around the waistband from about 2" (5cm) away from the left front edge continuing around to the right side seam.

6. Stitch on the Jet Beads: Pin the beaded trim to the bottom of the left waistband at the center front and continue around the waistband to 2½" (6.5cm) beyond the center back belt loop. (I needed 20" (51cm) of beaded trim for my project.) Baste and remove the pins. Hand-sew with running stitch and black embroidery floss.

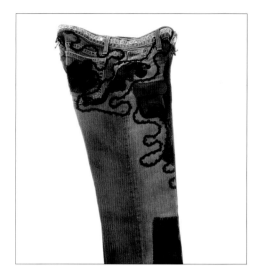

7. Stitch on the Burgundy Picot Ribbon: Pin the ribbon along the left side seam. Baste, remove pins, and sew around the perimeter with whipstitch and black embroidery floss.

8. Appliqué the Velvet Knee Patch: Pin the velvet to the right knee. Baste, remove pins, and whipstitch around the perimeter with brown embroidery floss.

9. Remove All Basting. Dry clean only.

YOUR CHALLENGE

Take a denim fitted skirt and convert it into a flirty, flippy, plaid skirt. This is a skirt for swooshing, dancing, or skipping; it's the girl-next-door look, done up with nonchalant denim cool. So get out your sewing basket and measuring tools to mark, pin, cut, sew, and recycle a boring skirt into this super look.

Then make a wide "it" belt to emphasize your waist with style. Your first step is to find an oversized buckle—an extravagant one, chunky and important. Match it with just the right shade of denim, and cut, pin, and sew, to create yourself a new belt.

schoolgirl charm skirt & waist cincher

schoolgirl charm skirt & waist cincher

How Difficult?

Intermediate. The sewing is basic—straight seams—but sewing them with precision takes patience, and the number of seams adds up to a lot of time. Allow a day to complete this project. Plaids should match along the pattern repeats; if doing so will cause you angst, substitute a floral- or paisley-printed wool. This project needs beautiful sewing to achieve the right look.

What Denim Do I Need?

You need a jean skirt that fits slimly around the bum with a fitted waist. The body should be pretty clean without a lot of details. I used a 100 percent cotton, slightly washed indigo skirt from Levi Strauss & Co., size 29. My skirt is cut straight, which makes it easier to figure the math in step 2, but if your skirt is flared it will also adapt beautifully. For the hip band you need two denim strips. Measure your hips 7" (18cm) below the waistline and add 8" (20.5cm) to the measurement. If you are Extra Small then measure from 6" (15cm) or 8" (20.5cm) for Extra Large and adjust the measurements through out accordingly. Divide that measurement by 2 to get the length of the strips. The width of the strips should be 3½" (9cm).

What Other Materials Will I Need?

Your "Sewing Basket"
(page 11)

Sewing machine

Denim blue thread

1 yard (1m) of a high-quality lightweight worsted wool plaid in navy, white, and red

2 1¼" (3cm) diameter red retro buttons

Red embroidery floss

school girl charm skirt

HOW TO DO IT STEP BY STEP

1. **Cut the Skirt Length:** Cut the skirt length to 24" (61cm), measuring from the bottom of the waistband. (Or cut it to the final length you want.)

If you are a beginner, make a simpler version—insert only 1 panel aligned down the right front thigh. If you are a couturier seamstress, make your skirt more elaborate by cutting your inserts on the bias and increasing the skirt length to mid-calf.

2. **Mark the Plaid Panel Inserts:** Lay the skirt flat. Measure the bottom width at the hem of the skirt and divide it by 12. (My skirt measured 36" (91cm), so 36 divided by 12 gave me 3—which meant that I inserted a plaid wool panel every 3" (7.5cm) at the hem.) Then measure the hip width of the skirt, 7" (18cm) from the bottom of the waistline (or adjust as explained left), and divide that measurement by 12. (My skirt had a straight side seam, so my hip also measured 36" (91cm); the plaid panels were inserted every 3" (7.5cm) at the hips just like at the

diagram 1

hem.) Once you have your measurements, mark the inserts on your skirt at the hem and at the hips. Following **diagram 1,** with tailor's chalk, mark every 3" (7.5cm) (or your measurement) along the hem, starting with a panel (3" (7.5cm) wide in my case) centered at the front hem. Mark the hips in the same manner, 7" (18cm) from the bottom of the waistline (or adjust as explained above) With a yardstick, connect your 2 marks with a straight chalk line, from the hip to the hem. You now have 12 lines on your skirt. Cut along the chalk lines. With denim blue thread, machine zigzag stitch the cut edges. Press.

3. **Cut the Plaid Panels:** Cut 12 rectangle shapes out of the plaid, each 7" wide x 18" long (18cm x 45.5cm) or the length of your denim skirt slashes + 1" (2.5cm).

Be careful when cutting the plaid—ensure that the plaid repeat will be exactly the same on each panel.

Finish the cut edge with a machine zigzag stitch along the 17" (43cm) edge, across the next 7" (18cm) edge, and down the other 17" (43cm) edge—leaving the last 7" (18cm) edge raw. The bottom edge will be your hem, and you will finish it later. Press on the wrong side.

4. **Sew the Plaid Inserts:** Following **diagram 2**, place the skirt and 1 plaid rectangle on a flat surface, with right sides up, and align the raw edge of the plaid with the hem of the skirt. With the right sides together, pin one long edge of the plaid rectangle to the adjacent slashed denim edge, from the hem to near the top of the slash. Pin the other side of the plaid rectangle to the other side of the slash in the same way. Baste and remove the pins. Sew the 2 seams with a ⅜" (1cm) allowance from the hem to within ½" (13mm) of the top of the slash. Repeat for each insert. Press all seams open on the wrong side. At the top of the slash, pull the excess plaid material through to the wrong side of the jeans and, following **diagram 3,** fold it into a double box pleat. Pin the pleats in place. Baste and remove the pins. Repeat for each insert. Then sew a double row of machine stitching around the hip, securely tacking each pleat in place. Remove the basting. Press the stitching lines. Machine zigzag stitch the hem all the way around. Press the hem on the wrong side.

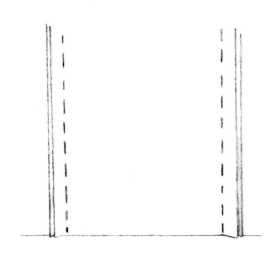

diagram 2

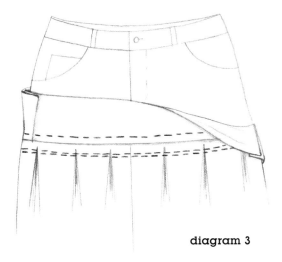

diagram 3

5. Make the Hip Band: With blue thread, machine zigzag stitch all around the edges of each denim hip band strip. Following **diagram 3,** pin 1 band to the skirt front ½" (13mm) above the stitch line, right sides together. Pin the other piece to the skirt back in the same way, having the back band overlap the front band. Baste, remove the pins, and machine stitch the denim hip band with ½" (13mm) seam allowance. Press the stitched seam, then fold the hip band down so it lies smoothly over the tucked plaid panels.

5. Sew on the Buttons: With red embroidery floss, sew a button to the hip band at each overlap.

waist cincher

How Difficult?

Beginner. Takes half an hour, max.

What Denim Do I Need?

A piece of denim 4½" (11.5cm) wide and as long as your waist measurement plus the extra length for your buckle. (I added an additional 6" (15cm) extra length for my buckle.) I am a size Medium. If you are extra petite or extra large you may want to adjust, reduce, or enlarge the belt width.

What Other Materials Will I Need?

Your "Sewing Basket" (page 11)

Oversized buckle; I used a 2½" x 4" (6.5cm x 10cm) hammered wood, two-piece interlocking buckle with brass trim

Sewing machine

Denim blue thread

HOW TO DO IT STEP BY STEP

1. **Fray the Denim:** Machine wash and dry the denim to softly fray the edges. Press.

2. **Attach the Buckle:** Slip the denim through the left side of the buckle and fold the end back 3" (7.5cm). The denim will gather at the buckle. Pin, baste, remove pins, and machine stitch in place. Holding the belt around your waist, slip the other end of the denim through the right side of the buckle, pull the end to fit your waist. Trim the overlap to 3" (7.5cm). Pin, baste, remove pins, and machine stitch in place. Everyone will have a different buckle, so adjust the overlap to your buckle. The key is to make it secure with an overlap long enough so that you have room to easily stitch it closed.

YOUR CHALLENGE

Make poor-man's jewelry by recycling old, one-of-a-kind buttons into hip denim patches that can be used to accessorize backpacks, jean pockets, belts, dresses, or jackets—patched on, pinned as a brooch, or even worn in the hair. Gather a bunch of wonderful vintage buttons in different shades, textures, sizes, and colors, then play with the arrangement and stitch them to denim patches. Surprise yourself!

toreador style patches on vest

toreador style patches

How Difficult?

Beginner. You just need to be able to sew on a button. It takes about half an hour to make one. For this project, make 2 of each shape—the square and the octagon. An has patches on her velvet cropped vest. Isabelle wears one in her hair on page 79. Isabelle's is heart-shaped backed with a matching piece of denim with quilt batting sandwiched in between for body. It's finished with a whip stitch edging and a barrette stitched to the back. Stitch on a safety pin instead to use it as a brooch. Just start making them. You're bound to love them, and find many ways to use them!

What Denim Do I Need?

A few scraps in assorted faded colors.

What Other Materials Will I Need?

Your "Sewing Basket" (page 11)

Photocopy of Octagon pattern (page 119)

Interesting vintage buttons

Lime, lilac, olive, and brown embroidery floss

HOW TO DO IT STEP BY STEP

1. **Cut the Denim:** Cut two each using the Hexagon pattern, and two 2½" (6.5cm) squares. Machine wash, dry, and press.

2. **Sew on the Buttons:** Play with them! Lay the buttons on the denim patches and see how colors change depending on what they are placed next to. See what happens when you use contrasting colors or colors that blend, making shapes pop or recede. Check out the photos of my samples for inspiration. Play around with the embroidery floss choice, in either a complementing or contrasting color—this is another opportunity to add texture and to express yourself. I used lime thread with the green buttons, pale lilac thread with the rust buttons, and brown buttons and olive thread with the red buttons. Hand-sew your buttons on with a continuous strand of embroidery floss, knotting securely after each button.

3. **Attach your Patches:** Pin the brooches on your chosen garment, try it on, and check the position. Adjust if necessary. Baste, remove pins, and with brown embroidery floss, whipstitch around the perimeter of each patch. Remove basting.

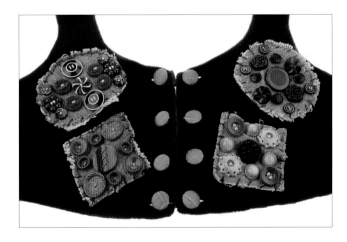

YOUR CHALLENGE

This project was inspired by an authentic Rider jacket and Lee jeans. They have a wonderful integrity, with signature details, unique stitching, and lots of gentle wear and tear. Adding exotic trims makes a glam play on London's Saville Row style. The pants in this project are designed symmetrically except for a splash of buttons on the right pocket, and the design on the jacket is asymmetrical—the balance is key to the DR allure. The trims need to be luxe, so find beautiful ecru cotton laces—ones intended for pretty blouses. Combine these with black silk and velvet accents as well as black and white buttons. The trims have a groovy vintage appeal, not unlike the Lee detailing.

Bonne chance!

saville row bespoke suit

saville row bespoke suit

How Difficult?

Intermediate. The hand- and machine-sewing are basic, but it will take a weekend to attach all the trims and properly jazz up the clothes. This project requires patience and a love of sewing. You'll need to maneuver to get your hands into the pant legs to sew on the trims, so persevere. The workmanship needs to be fine on this project, so don't rush it. In the end, you'll have an heirloom outfit as well as the satisfaction of crafting it yourself.

What Denim Do I Need?

Matching jacket and jeans. I used the Gold Label Lee Rider jacket in size 10 and Lee jeans style 101B in size 28W 33L, both in 100 percent faded cotton.

What Other Materials Will I Need?

Your "Sewing Basket" (page 11)

7" x 40" (18cm x 101cm) piece of black silk velvet or twice the width of the cuffs plus 1½" (3.8cm)

Sewing machine

Black, ochre, ecru, cream, and denim thread

Cream embroidery floss

60" (150cm) of 1" (2.5cm) 100 percent cotton vintage French lace ribbon in ecru

60" (150cm) of 1" (2cm) 100 percent cotton vintage French lace ribbon in ecru

10 decorative 100 percent cotton lace collar and blouse insert pieces in ecru

Using my lace trims as a guide, search for ones that appeal to you. There are many lace appliqués for decorating blouses that look hip and new applied to denim.

Assortment of black and ivory buttons, plastic and shell

6" x 20" (15cm x 51cm) piece of black silk taffeta

HOW TO DO IT STEP BY STEP

1. **Jazz up the Jean Cuffs:** Measure your jean cuff width and cut a 7" (18cm) wide piece of velvet the length of your cuff plus 1½" (3.8cm). Machine zigzag stitch around the perimeter of the velvet with black thread. Fold the strip in half with right sides together and pin a seam. Baste, remove pins, and machine stitch with a ½" (13mm) seam allowance to form a tube. Using a pressing cloth, carefully steam the seam open on the wrong side with the iron held above the pressing cloth.

Lay the velvet around the jean cuff, with the velvet seam aligned with the jean inseam and the velvet edge aligned with the jean cuff edge. Gently smooth the velvet and pin it over the denim. Baste along the top velvet edge and remove the pins. Thread your machine with black thread in the top spool and ochre in the bobbin, and sew so that the ochre is on the denim and the black is on the velvet. Machine zigzag along the top and bottom edges of the velvet. Repeat on the other cuff.

Pin the 1" (2.5cm) wide lace ribbon over the bottom of the cuff. Join the lace with a ½" (13mm) overlap at the inseam. Baste and remove the pins. Machine topstitch the lace around the perimeter. Repeat with the ¾" (2cm) lace at the top edge of the velvet. Repeat on the other cuff.

2. Attach the Lace Appliqués to the Jeans: Lay the jeans flat and arrange the various lace shapes. Play with them—move the lace around, stepping back so you can get a different perspective. Make your arrangement of the lace symmetrical on both jean legs. When you are satisfied with the arrangement, pin the laces down, and try the jeans on. Adjust the placement if necessary. Once you are content, baste, and remove the pins. Sew the appliqués on by hand with cream thread. It takes time to sew them all on by hand, but it can be a cool travel project! I sewed with a whipstitch around the perimeters and a bit of running stitch to tack inside the larger appliqués.

3. Sew on the Buttons: Arrange the buttons in a splash over the right pocket lace appliqué. I literally just dropped them on the jeans. Once you have an arrangement you like, mark each button's place with tailor's chalk and set the buttons aside in the same order. Sew them on with a continuous piece of cream embroidery floss, knotting securely after each button.

4. Make a Back Pant Label: Cut a 3" x 2¼" (7.5cm x 5.5cm) rectangle from the velvet and pin to the back waist. Baste, remove the pins, and machine zigzag stitch the label all around the edges with black thread. Remove the basting.

5. Make the Black Silk Jacket Appliqué: Machine zig-zag stitch with black thread all around the edges of the black silk piece. Following the **diagram** to the right, fold pleats along the length of the silk ¾" (2cm) deep and ¾" (2cm) apart. Baste, remove the pins, and machine-sew the pleats in place 1" (2.5cm) from each edge. Pin the pleated silk on the right shoulder of the jacket. Try it on and look in the mirror to check the placement. Adjust if necessary. Baste and remove pins. Thread black thread in the top spool and ochre thread in the bobbin and stitch in place around perimeter, 1" (2.5cm) from outside edge with the black thread on the silk and ochre on the denim.

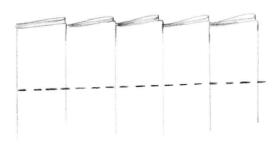

6. Apply the Laces to the Jacket: As you did with the jeans, place the jacket flat and just play with the laces until you love the look. For the jacket, position the appliqués asymmetrically to contrast with the symmetrical placement on the jeans. Try it on and adjust if necessary. Baste, remove pins, and hand-sew the appliqués in place with cream thread as you did on the jeans.

7. Sew the Buttons on the Jacket: You need to scatter buttons on the shoulders and the right collar point. Arrange the buttons, mark their positions and sew them in place as you did for the jeans in step 3.

Dry clean only.

YOUR CHALLENGE

Play sophisticated textures and patterns against the simplicity of rugged denim. This charming cropped jacket, full of hard-wearing splendor—both upscale and campy—is the *it* look. Get your design juices flowing to give Downtown Babe that chic attitude, that note of confidence, that *savoir faire*.

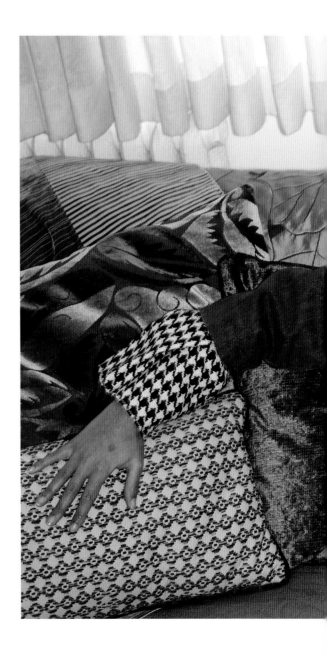

jacket

downtown babe jacket

How Difficult?

Experienced. Some machine- and hand-sewing skill is necessary. Attention to detail and a desire to design and play with fabrics are crucial to achieving a professional finish. Be patient and finish the details just right—fine crafting is key to this look. Allow a full day to complete the project.

What Denim Do I Need?

The jacket I used for this project is a size smaller than I generally wear because I wanted a slightly slimmer fit. Choose a jacket that fits you the way you like. Mine is labeled Divided which is a brand available in H&M stores worldwide. It's Western style in a sturdy, stonewashed 100 percent cotton. The shade looks great with black and white checks.

What Other Materials Will I Need

Your "Sewing Basket" (page 11)

½ yard (45cm) of cream and black houndstooth check woolen fabric

Sewing machine

Cream thread

Burgundy embroidery floss

Photocopy of Downtown Babe Collar pattern (page 121)

⅓ yard (30cm) floral-print silk charmeuse

⅓ yard (30cm) glen plaid check worsted wool fabric

10 black and silver assorted gorgeous buttons ½" (13mm)–¾" (2cm) in diameter

HOW TO DO IT STEP BY STEP

1. **Reshape the Jacket:** Following **diagram 1,** mark the cutting line with tailor's chalk. We will all be working with different jackets and have different body shapes so use my measurements as a guide, and reduce or increase proportionately to fit as necessary. After you have marked the jacket, try it on, and if necessary, adjust the cutting line to be more flattering for your size. Then lay the jacket on the table. If you made adjustments, reshape the revised cutting line, with tailor's chalk. Double-check your measurements. Are your side seams exactly the same measurements? Is the left front exactly the same as the right front? Are the sleeves the exact same length? Small differences can make the jacket look glaringly crooked, so spend time to make it symmetrical. Then cut the new shape. Machine wash, dry, and press.

diagram 1

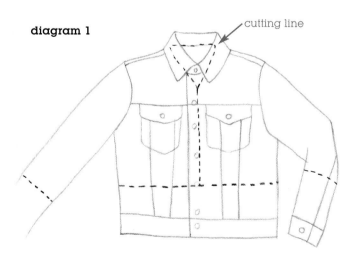

cutting line

2. Make the Cuffs: Cut two 8" x 21" (20.5cm x 53.5cm) pieces from the houndstooth check.

When cutting houndstooth, pay attention to the check pattern. Cut straight along the checks. The bold pattern will magnify any imperfection in the cutting or sewing, so take your time and develop your designer eye!

Machine zigzag stitch all around the edges of the houndstooth pieces. Press with a pressing cloth. Sew the side seam together with ⅝" (15mm) seam allowance to make two cuffs. Using a pressing cloth, press the seam open on the wrong side of the material. Align the seam of one houndstooth cuff with the inside seam of one jacket sleeve. Pin the houndstooth to the sleeve, with the denim overlapping the houndstooth by 1½" (3.8cm). Following **diagram 2,** fold the excess houndstooth material into a box pleat on the top of the cuff as shown. Baste seam and remove pins. Using the embroidery floss, double topstitch with running stitch, 1" (2.5cm) and ¾" (2cm) from the denim edge. Remove basting. Gently press from the wrong side, protecting the fabric with a pressing cloth. Repeat for the other cuff.

diagram 2

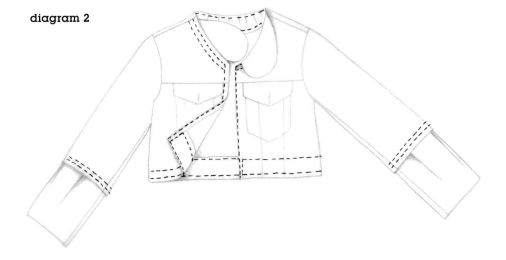

3. **Make the Collar:** Using the Downtown Babe Collar pattern, cut 2 each of the houndstooth and the silk floral collar pieces, flipping the pattern so you have a left and right collar.

With wrong sides together, pin 1 piece of silk to one piece of houndstooth, baste, and remove the pins. Gently machine-sew all around the edge in zigzag stitch. The collar is cut on the bias, as indicated on the pattern, making it very elastic, so be careful not to stretch it out of shape as you sew. Remove the basting. Repeat with the other collar pieces. Gently press using a pressing cloth.

4. **Sew the Collar to the Jacket:** Following **diagram 3,** (pin the collar on the jacket, 1" (2.5cm) from center front edge, with a 1" (2.5cm) overlap on the neckline. Baste and remove the pins. With burgundy embroidery floss, secure the collar with 2 rows of running stitch, ½" (13mm) and 1" (2.5cm) from the collar edge. Remove the basting.

5. **Add a Hem Facing:** Following **diagram 2,** cut the glen plaid into a 2" x 36" (5cm x 91cm) long strip. Finish all around the edges with a machine zigzag stitch in cream thread. Pin it to the inside of the jacket along the lower edge, folding it under ⅝" (15mm) at the jacket front edges and cutting off any excess. Baste and remove the pins. Hand-sew with burgundy embroidery floss in two lines of running stitch, ⅜" (1cm) and 1¾" (4.5cm) from jacket hem edge. Remove basting.

Before you cut your gorgeous materials, check the collar size on your jacket by cutting a collar out of a denim scrap. Pin it on your jacket and check to see if it fits the size of your front neck edge. If necessary, adjust the collar pattern size.

diagram 3

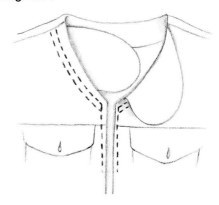

6. **Add a Neck Facing:** Cut the glen plaid into a 2" x 30" (5cm x 76cm) long strip. Finish all around the edges with a machine zigzag stitch in cream thread. Pin it from shoulder seam to shoulder seam around the back neck—note that because this is curved, you will need to add a few small tucks to the fabric around the neck edge so that the outer edge of the facing will lie flat. (I needed to add 6 tucks, ¼" (6mm) deep each.). Baste, remove pins and hand sew with running stitch and burgundy embroidery floss 1½" and ½" (3.8cm x 13mm) from the edge as shown.

7. **Make a Back Neck Patch:** See photo of back view. Cut out one 3" x 2⅜" (7.5cm x 6cm) piece each from the houndstooth and the silk floral. With wrong sides together, pin, baste, remove pins, and machine zigzag stitch all around the edges, careful not to stretch the material. Gently press using a pressing cloth. Using burgundy embroidery floss, sew the back neck patch to the center back neckline following the interfacing stitching line.

8. **Finish the Center Front:** With burgundy embroidery floss, hand-stitch a running stitch ⅜" (1cm) from the center front edge, from neck to hem as illustrated in **diagrams 2 and 3.**

9. **Sew on the Buttons:** Create a pretty corsage on the collars with your buttons. Make them a bit whimsical—gently balanced yet not perfectly matched. Sew the buttons on with a continuous thread, knotting securely after each button. Remove the tack buttons on the front pockets.

10. **Final Jacket Finish:** Press carefully on the wrong side, using a pressing cloth to avoid damage to the wool, silk, and hand-stitching. Dry clean only.

mod bag of spring tricks

Take delicious, sweet, fresh pinks, aquamarines, and rugged denim blues and mix it up with flowers, hearts, buttons, animal spots, and shiny sparklers to add some lively punch to your spring look.

YOUR CHALLENGE

Have DR fun whipping up this funky, button-spiced mini-skirt. It's a groovy Kings Road look from the '60s. Your challenge is to search for interesting, oversized vintage buttons—then it's fun and games to decide on how to place them.

daddy-o

daddy-o miniskirt

How Difficult?

Beginner. You only need to be able to sew on a button!

What Denim Do I Need?

A 100 percent cotton jean skirt, the sturdy, basic type. Mine has an oversized waistband, a zipper, topstitching, and loop details that emphasize the big, oversized theme of this project. Check out Convert a Pair of Jeans into a Denim Skirt (page 117) to make your own skirt.

What Other Materials Will I Need?

Your "Sewing Basket" (page 11)

Lots of big blue and green vintage buttons—I used 26 buttons that varied in size from ⅝" (15mm) to 2" (5cm) in diameter

Denim blue embroidery floss

HOW TO DO IT STEP BY STEP

1. **Cut the Skirt Length:** Cut your skirt to a mini length, or as desired. My finished skirt, size Medium, measures 14" (35.5cm) long from the natural waistline. Machine wash, dry, and press.

2. **Sew on the Buttons:** Lay the skirt flat, front side up. Arrange the buttons on the skirt in a balanced layout. With tailor's chalk, place a mark under each button, then place the buttons aside, keeping them in the same layout. Sew the buttons in place with the embroidery floss, securing each button separately. Repeat for the skirt back, then fill in any gaps on the sides.

Be certain that your buttons have been very securely sewn on and that the threads are well-knotted so you can machine wash the skirt without losing any buttons! Since I used vintage buttons, I turn the skirt inside out and throw it into a lingerie bag when I wash it.

YOUR CHALLENGE

Add color and personal
attitude to your look by
recycling men's ties into your
new favorite accoutrement:
a denim tie-belt or a scarf
to tie onto a belt loop or wear
around your neck. It's an
anything-goes, young at
heart accessory.

funky tie-all scarf

funky tie-all scarf

How Difficult?

Easy. Takes less than 1 hour. You need a bit of machine sewing experience.

What Denim Do I Need?

A pant leg from a faded, softly worn pair of jeans, plus a belt loop.

What Other Materials Will I Need?

Your "Sewing Basket"(page 11)

Sewing machine

Denim blue thread

Silk tie with a funky print

Silk thread in a color that blends with your tie's main color

Be careful not to stretch your tie when you cut, as it is on the bias and the shape can easily become distorted.

Machine wash and dry a delicate tie!? Good quality silks have been properly dyed, and like denim, the color will fade with washing rather than run—and that effect will be lovely for this project. Do a test, and wash the discarded portion of the tie before you wash your project. It's your DR call—do you like the results?

HOW TO DO IT STEP BY STEP

1. **Cut the Denim:** Cut the pant leg along the side seam. Now you have a flat piece of fabric. Press. With a yard-stick and tailor's chalk, mark 3 strips, each ½" (13mm) wider than the widest point of your tie and as long as possible. My strips were 3½" wide x 20" long (9cm x 51cm).

2. **Sew the Denim:** Now you will form one long strip of denim from your 3 pieces. Lay one denim piece right side up on the table. Lay the next piece right side up as an extension of it, with a ⅝" (15mm) overlap. Pin, baste, and remove the pins. Trim the overlap neatly if necessary and then machine sew down the middle of the overlap with the denim thread. Repeat with the third strip.

3. **Cut Your Tie:** Carefully cut all the way along the outer folded edge of the tie. Keep only the top layer of the silk. Discard the back of the tie.

4. **Assemble the Tie:** Lay the silk on the denim, wrong sides together, and pin together with the denim joinings distributed as evenly as possible. Baste together down the center of the two pieces and remove the pins. Cut the denim even with the edge of the silk. Thread denim thread in the bobbin and silk thread in the top spool. Machine-sew the layers together ¼" (6mm) from the edge, all around the perimeter with the silk thread on the silk fabric. Remove the basting. Hand-sew the denim belt loop on the back of the tie, 4" (10cm) from front tip as shown in the photo, using denim thread and catching only the denim.

5. **Fray the Denim:** Machine wash in cold water and dry to get the nice frayed denim edges. Take care to not damage the tie silk.

6. **Press.**

YOUR CHALLENGE

Catch the sweet mood of spring with these wonderful pedal pushers! Trimmed with a variety of textures and sunburst attitude, they radiate little-girl style. Keep the trims light and flirty and try on the jeans as you work, adding this and that here and there. The trick is to find a variety of textures—a floral ribbon, a red plaid, pink and turquoise checks, red buttons, lots of rugged denim scraps, and printed flowers to give your signature pedal pushers an energy all your own.

alice in wonderland pedal pushers

alice in wonderland pedal pushers

How Difficult?

Intermediate. You will hand-sew, machine-sew, cut out templates, and sew on buttons—this project features bits of all the sewing crafts. Allow a day or two to complete this project.

What Denim Do I Need?

A pair of faded jeans that fit your bum snugly and grip your legs. You also need a few denim scraps in contrasting colors.

What Other Materials Will I Need?

Your "Sewing Basket" (page 11)

About 18" x 18" (45cm x 45cm) square of red and navy plaid fabric

Photocopy of Petal pattern (page 120)

Photocopy of Heart pattern (page 119)

Sewing machine

Ochre thread

12" x 12" (30cm x 30cm) square of pink and white cotton gingham

Denim blue, lime, red, pink, yellow, turquoise, and coral embroidery floss

10 assorted blue and green vintage buttons

1 yard (1m) of 1" (2.5cm) wide red floral cotton ribbon

½ yard (50cm) of 1" (2.5cm) wide turquoise checked ribbon

½ yard (50cm) of cotton fabric with pretty printed flowers to cut out and scatter on the pants (I used a home-furnishing fabric, which is sturdier than fine dressmaker fabric and better suited to this project)

6" x 6" (15cm x 15cm) square of beige and red check cotton fabric

HOW TO DO IT STEP BY STEP

1. **Cut the Length:** Try the jeans on to decide the right length—with the cuff rolled back twice, the jeans should hover around the knee. With tailor's chalk, mark the desired length with the cuff unrolled, and cut. My jeans, in a size Medium, are cut 29" (74cm) long.

2. **Add a Plaid Daisy:** Cut 5 petals from the red and navy plaid using the Petal pattern. Machine zigzag stitch around the outside of each petal with ochre thread. Press. For the flower center, cut a circle, 3" (7.5cm) in diameter, from a scrap of darker denim. Pin 5 petals and flower center to the right thigh of the jeans below the front pocket opening as shown in the photo. The flower should wrap around your thigh, so position it so that 2 petals overlap the side seam to the back of the leg and the flower center and the other 3 petals are on the front of the leg. Baste, remove the pins, and, with denim blue embroidery floss, hand-sew a running stitch around each petal, ¼" (6mm) from the edge. With lime embroidery floss and blanket stitch, sew the flower denim center in place. Embellish it with 5 embroidered stars in red embroidery floss. With denim embroidery floss, add a chain stitch around the circle, ½" (13mm) from the edge. With lime embroidery floss, embroider stars to fill in the gaps between the petals. Remove basting.

3. **Add a Love Patch:** Print out the word *love* on a computer. I used font Berlin Sans FB, 250 pt, bold, outlined. Pin the word to the cotton gingham on the bias. Cut the letters out of the cotton gingham and pin them to a scrap of faded denim in a fun arrangement. Baste, remove pins, and, with ochre thread, machine zigzag stitch around the perimeters of each letter. Trim the denim around the group of letters with a ½" (13mm) border. Pin the patch to the left back of the jeans, overlapping the waistband and crossing the back pocket. Machine zigzag stitch with ochre thread ¼" (6mm) from the denim edge and down the center of the patch. Then jazz the patch up with embroidery. I embellished it with feather-stitching around the perimeter with pink embroidery floss halfway around and then switched to red. I used turquoise embroidery floss to add some cross stitches to highlight the letter "O" and some yellow embroidery floss daisies to fill some empty spaces.

4. **Appliqué a Denim Heart:** Cut a heart out of a piece of faded denim using the Heart pattern on page 119. In a random arrangement sew the buttons onto the heart with lime embroidery floss. Use a continuous thread and knot securely after each button. Pin the heart to the left front, angled and just below the top edge of the pocket. Baste, remove pins, and with pink embroidery floss, stitch the heart to the left back pocket with cross-stitch. Further highlight the heart by sewing a running stitch on the jeans around the outside edge.

5. **Sew on the Ribbons:** Pin the red floral ribbon to the jean front with the ribbon edge aligned with the left jean side seam. Baste, remove pins, and with denim embroidery floss and running stitch, sew to the jeans around the perimeter. Pin the turquoise gingham ribbon to the jean back with the edge aligned with the floral ribbon. Baste, remove pins, and with coral embroidery floss and blanket stitch, sew to the jeans around the perimeter. My turquoise ribbon was only 13" (33cm) long, so I centered it along the length of the floral ribbon. Do your DR thing, and recyle and improvise with what you have or love!

6. **Add some Denim Patches:** Referring to the photo, pin the worn knee patch to the left knee, a denim scrap diagonally to the right lower leg, a third scrap down the center of the left back leg, and a fourth patch diagonally to the right back pocket. Try on the jeans and check the placement. Baste, remove pins, and with running stitch sew the patches in place ¼" (6mm) from the edge around the perimeter. For the 2 front patches, I used denim embroidery floss and for the rear patches I used yellow embroidery floss on the left leg and red floss on the back pocket.

7. **Appliqué a Plaid Patch:** Add the beige and red check cotton fabric patch on the left inseam. It should be pinned on a diagonal, wrapping to the back. Baste, remove pins, and blanket stitch around the perimeter with turquoise embroidery floss.

8. **Appliqué the Printed Flowers:** Cut several printed flowers out of the cotton fabric. Scatter them on the jeans and play with the arrangement. Overlap the flowers on one of the plaid daisy petals, on the check patch, and on the denim knee patch to pull the look together. I patched the prettiest flower on the right rear bum because jeans need to look great from the rear, too. Give it that breezy DR styling! Pin the flowers in place, try the jeans on, and check the look from the front, sides, and rear. Adjust the positioning of the flowers if necessary. Baste, remove pins, and whipstitch the flowers in place with embroidery floss, alternating between lime and pink. Finally, add embroidery stitches in various colors for texture

9. **Machine wash and dry this project in cold water;** the wear will add to the lovely effect of the design.

rhinestone pocket pouch

YOUR CHALLENGE

Create a funky yet functional "A-List" belt bag to store and carry your most important gear. Recycle denim, add a gorgeous button, and you have an ultra hip and quick fashion fix!

rhinestone pocket pouch

rhinestone pocket pouch

How Difficult?

Beginner. This great beginner project takes just a bit of sewing, cutting, and pressing—then it's done. It takes about half an hour, so step up to the design podium and do your thing—the project will work whatever your ability.

What Denim Do I Need?

A back jean pocket and denim scraps for the belt loops and the pocket flap, all in basic 100 percent cotton denim.

What Other Materials Will I Need?

Your "Sewing Basket" (page 11)

Photocopy of Pocket Flap pattern (page 122)

7" x 7" (18cm x 18cm) square of white iron-on interfacing

Ochre embroidery floss

1" (2.5cm) diameter vintage rhinestone button

1" (2.5cm) diameter silver metal key ring

2½" (6.5cm) long silver metal snap bolt

HOW TO DO IT STEP BY STEP

1. **Cut the Denim:** Cut one back pocket off a pair of jeans, cutting neatly around the outside finished edge of the pocket, with the back side intact. Cut the Pocket Flap pattern from a denim scrap. Cut 2 denim belt loops out of the denim scrap, each 1" x 6" (2.5cm x 15cm). Machine wash, dry, and then press the pieces.

Your jean pocket won't necessarily be the exact same size as mine, so check the flap pattern and make it a bit wider or narrower if necessary.

2. **Interface the Flap:** Cut the pocket flap interfacing as indicated on the Pocket Flap pattern on page 122. Then place the interfacing on the denim, positioned as marked on the pattern, with the glue side of the interfacing against the wrong side of the denim. Following the product instructions, adhere the interfacing to the denim.

3. **Assemble the Pocket:** Pin the flap to the back side of the pocket as shown in the photo. Baste, remove the pins, and with ochre embroidery floss and backstitch, join the two pieces ⅜" (1cm) in from the edge. Sew the raw edges together with blanket stitch. Remove the basting.

4. **Make the Buttonhole:** Mark a buttonhole on the flap following the position marked on the Pocket Flap pattern, adjusting the length if necessary to the diameter of your button. The length should be the diameter of your button plus ⅛" (3mm). Cut the buttonhole, align the button, and sew the button firmly to the pocket with ochre embroidery floss.

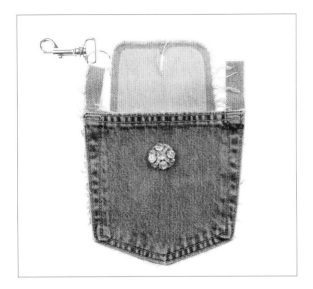

5. **Attach the Belt Loops:** Fold a belt loop in half and sew securely with a few hand stitches to the back side of the pocket, overlapping the top edge by 1" (2.5cm). Repeat with the remaining loop on the opposite side.

6. **Add a Snap Bolt:** Attach the key ring to one belt loop and cinch on a snap bolt. Slip a belt or scarf through the belt loops to wear this belt bag, or like Isabelle, clip the snap bolt on the other belt loop to carry it as a small bag.

YOUR CHALLENGE

These short-shorts are for show
and tell! It's time to show off
your toned and tan legs with
these super-high-cut jeans.
You will make them savage,
with a fringed denim edge
to the cuff and lots of jet-set
baubles, chains, jewels, and
fur pocket flaps. It's an easy-
to-do, golden-splendor, all-out
denim glamour!

ring my bell super-short shorts

ring my bell
super-short shorts

How Difficult?

Easy. You just need to be able to cut and do a wee bit of sewing. It takes a couple of hours. This can be a good beginner project! The elements are so fabulous together that the project works whatever your skill level. I list all the doodads that I attached to the jeans. Use it as a guide when you search for trims to define your look along with whatever else you have available.

What Denim Do I Need?

A pair of old, worn jeans that fit snug on the bum in basic 100 percent cotton.

What Other Materials Will I Need?

Your "Sewing Basket" (page 11)

Sewing machine

Ochre thread

Two 4" x 5" (10cm x 12.5cm) pieces of faux fur

Denim blue embroidery floss

Gold, pearl, and rhinestone buttons and sew on beads—I used 28 in total

6 gold shank buttons, ¾" (2cm) in diameter for the back fur pocket flaps

5" (12.5cm) long brown silk tassel

⅜" wide x 4" long (1cm x 10cm) gold chain

⅜" wide x 12" long (1cm x 30.5cm) silver chain

⅛" wide x 1 yard (3mm x 1m) copper chain

1" (2.5cm) vintage silver metal key ring

HOW TO DO IT STEP BY STEP

1. **Shape the Jeans:** Mark the jeans with tailor's chalk to cut as short as you dare. My sample has a 4" (10cm) side seam and a ½" (13mm) inseam, as shown in **diagram 1.** Try them on, adjust markings if necessary, then cut.

diagram 1

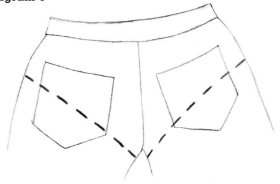

2. **Make the Cuff Fringe:** With tailor's chalk and a ruler, mark and cut two 2" x 36" (5cm x 91cm) denim strips from the front discarded legs of the jeans. Then cut 1" (2.5cm) deep cuts perpendicular to the length every ½" (13mm) along the strip to make your cuff fringe. Pin the fringe to the cuff of the shorts with the cuff edge overlapping the fringe by ¾" (2cm). Baste, remove the pins, and machine stitch down the center of the overlap with ochre thread. Repeat for the second cuff. Machine wash the shorts, dry, and press.

3. **Make the Back Pocket Fur Flaps:** Following **diagram 2,** tuck 1½" (3.8cm) of one of the fur pieces inside the right back pocket with the wrong side of the fur facing up. Pin the fur to the pocket. Baste, and remove the pins. Hand-sew it with running stitch and denim floss down the center of the overlap. Then fold the fur down over the front of the pocket and tack it in 3 places with dazzling shank buttons as shown in the photo. Repeat on the other pocket.

4. **Embellish the Shorts:** Play with the bling—the stones, chains, and jewels—until you are satisfied with the balance of the placement. Use what I did as inspiration. When you are satisfied with the balance, sew your bling on securely with a continuous thread, knotting after each button. Don't be boring or shy! Throw it all on, the more the merrier.

diagram 2

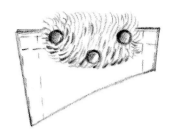

tarzan loves jane carryall bag

YOUR CHALLENGE

If Tarzan went shopping on Rodeo Drive in Beverly Hills, what bag would he buy Jane? Your challenge is to create Jane's dream bag. It's got gold, leopard print, and rhinestones—the most luxurious possibilities patched on top of old, worn denim. It's a big carryall sack, a colorful cocktail of textures and cheeky nonchalance. So step up to the plate, find the fabulous trims, and make a big beautiful carryall bag as unique as you and your fashion sense!

tarzan loves jane carryall bag

tarzan loves jane carryall bag

How Difficult?

Intermediate. It's a fun patchwork project with no possibility for error because there is no right or wrong. All that's needed is an eclectic contrast of textures. You will need some machine and hand-sewing experience. Allow a day to make it.

What Denim Do I Need?

You need a variety of denim scraps and patches, from different jeans, all washed and faded. Take your I-Box to the sewing table and turn it upside down. Search through your pile of scraps to find just the right shapes and colors for the patchwork.

What Other Materials Will I Need?

Your "Sewing Basket" (page 11)

Sewing machine

Denim blue and black thread

Photocopy of Satchel pattern (page 120)

4" x 8" (10cm x 20.5cm) piece of graphic silk tie material

⅓ yard (30mm) iron-on interfacing

12" x 12" (30.5cm x 30.5cm) square of gold silk crushed velvet

Gold silk thread

17" x 10" (43 x 25.5cm) vintage spotted fur

8" x (20.5 x 23cm) metallic gold leather

12" (30.5cm) length of ½" (13mm) wide braid with a double row of rhinestones

2 vintage rhinestone buckles, 2" (5cm) wide

½ yard (46cm) blue rayon lining material

A piece of leopard skin I found in the corner of an old fabric shop became the inspiration for this project. Look at the photos and my trim list as a guide, then go hunting, and discover new or vintage "finds" that inspire you.

HOW TO DO IT STEP BY STEP

1. **Create the Denim Patchwork:** Lay the denim pieces flat, overlapping them in a patchwork fashion until you have a pleasing composition that measures approximately 17" x 21" (43cm x 53.5cm). While you work on your patchwork, keeping it smooth is key. You want to finish with a nice, flat piece of patched material. When you like the balance and texture, pin the patches in place. There should be at least a ½" (13mm) overlap of adjacent patches. Baste and remove the pins. Trim the outside edge of the joined piece to a rectangular shape; trim any oversized overlaps. Machine zigzag stitch the patches together with denim thread ¼" (6mm) from the edge. When you finish, turn the joined piece over and trim the overlaps on the backside to ½" (13mm). Pin the Satchel pattern onto the patchwork rectangle. Cut it out to make your bag front. Repeat for the bag back.

To get an interesting effect and add balance to the project, make each piece from 6 to 8 patches and include a couple of jean seams on the front and on the back. The denim has a grain line to it as well as a right and wrong side, so vary these characteristics—turn the material upside down, for example—to achieve a sophisticated mix of textures with whatever denim you have available.

2. **Cut the Shoulder Straps:** Cut two 2¾" x 30" (6.5cm x 76cm) denim strips. Cut one 2¾" x 20" (6.5cm x 51cm) denim strip. Machine wash and dry the shoulder straps and the bag body pieces to get nice frayed edges. Press each piece.

3. **Appliqué the Silk Patches:** Cut the silk tie and the interfacing. Steam the interfacing to the wrong side of the silk. Repeat for the silk velvet patch. Pin patches to the bag front. Baste, remove the pins, and machine zigzag stitch with gold silk thread all around the edges. Remove the basting.

4. **Assemble the Bag:** Mark, pin, and sew the darts on the wrong side with denim blue thread. Press the darts. Pin the front and back pieces of the bag with wrong sides together. Baste, remove pins, and machine zigzag stitch along the sides and bottom with denim blue thread, ½" (13mm) in from the outside edge.

5. **Attach the Fur and Gold Leather:** Pin the fur and gold leather swatches so they wrap around the side seams gracefully. Everyone's fur will be different shapes and sizes, so trust your DR style to find the right look. Thread gold silk thread in the top spool and denim in the bobbin. Machine zigzag stitch on the top and sides with gold silk thread on the fur.

6. **Sew on the Rhinestone Braid:** Pin the rhinestone braid in a gentle curve as shown in the photo. Baste, remove pins, and sew with black thread and running stitch around the perimeter.

If you are a bead whiz and want to add more glitter to the bag, bead a flower, an initial, or whatever you like instead of using the rhinestone braid (or in addition to it!)

7. Make the Shoulder Strap: The strap is made in three sections. For the center section, reinforce the 20" (51cm) denim strip with a 2½" x 12" (6.5cm x 30.5cm) piece of silk velvet. Interface the velvet (as for the patch in step 3). Pin it to the center of the strip. With gold silk thread in the top spool and denim thread in the bobbin, machine zigzag stitch around the perimeter of the velvet. Press. The velvet side is the inside of the strap. Join one of the 2 remaining denim strips to each end of the center section, as illustrated in the **diagram** below, slipping one end of each through a buckle and folding the end back 1" (2.5cm). Pin, baste, and remove pins. With denim thread, stitch the fold end in place and reinforce with machine topstitching as shown in the **diagram** below. Finally, tuck 2" of each strap end into the bag, centered at a side seam. Pin, baste, remove pins, and, with denim thread, machine topstitch around the perimeter of the bag top and around each 2" (5cm) strap end.

machine topstitch   zigzag stitch   machine topstitch

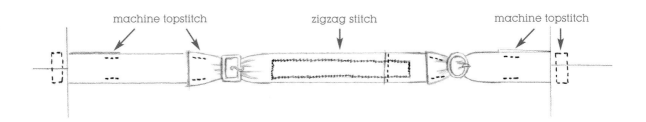

This is an oversized bag with an extra-long strap. Let it flow naturally. Depending on your denim and buckles, the measurements may change. Use mine only as a guide—you're recycling, building your satchel to suit your materials.

8. Line the Bag: Cut out 2 pieces of the rayon lining material using the Satchel pattern. Mark and sew the darts. With right sides together, pin and sew around the side and bottom edges with a ½" (13mm) seam allowance and denim blue thread. Finish the top edge with a machine zigzag stitch twice around. Press the seams open and press the whole piece. Insert the lining into the bag and pin it in place, with wrong sides of the lining and bag together. The lining should sit ½" (13mm) below the denim edge at the top opening. Pin in place, baste, remove the pins, and machine stitch with denim blue thread 1" (2.5cm) from the top opening. Remove the basting.

Press the top stitching line.

sweet pea

Summer on the Côte d'Azur is all about flaunting skin, style, and the latest hot fashions. Or maybe your compass points to another attitude, like a blissful summer in Bozeman, with the touch of sweet innocence. Whatever your look or dream vacation, infuse your wardrobe with your summer mood.

YOUR CHALLENGE

For this project, you will recycle a pair of jeans into a new, überlong denim skirt. The front and back inserts will be covered with fabulous denim patchwork. Your entire stock of denim leftovers will be scrutinized to choose the best ones for this "it" look. You will gussy it up further with tucks around the thighs so it snuggles the body and give it a touch of dramatic flair and petticoat attitude with pretty lace and blush silk stitched into the hem. This is over-the-top DR fashion, done up in Woodstock-style. This skirt is full of character—it's Janis Joplin belting out the blues; it's real; it's romantic and hip.

woodstock cool jean skirt

woodstock cool jean skirt

How Difficult?

Intermediate. The sewing is pretty basic; you only need to be able to sew a straight line by machine, but it takes time to rip out the jeans, remake them into a skirt, do the patchwork, and sew the faux-petticoat. You'll need patience and at least a day to make this project. It's a gorgeous look and if you love to sew, this project is for you.

What Denim Do I Need?

I used Heritage d'Amerique, size 36L 34W, 100 percent cotton. You also need a variety of denim scraps in different shades and textures, so take out your I-box.

What Other Materials Will I Need?

Your "Sewing Basket" (page 11)

Ochre and blush thread

1 yard (1m) blush silk georgette

3 yards (3m) of ¾" (2cm) wide of various lace trims

HOW TO DO IT STEP BY STEP

1. **Make the Skirt Shape:** Cut the jean cuffs off just above the hem and make the pants into a jean skirt, following the first paragraph of Convert a Pair of Jeans into a Denim Skirt on page 117. You will be left with a big V-shaped gap at the center front and back.

2. **Make the Patchwork Inserts:** Lay the skirt flat with the front side up. Select and arrange your denim scraps to form a patchwork insert to fill the front gap. Try for an interesting variety of textures. It's DR fun—there is no right or wrong, so enjoy the process! Once you are pleased with your insert, pin it together. The pieces should overlap each other by about 1" (2.5cm). Baste, remove the pins, and with ochre thread, machine stitch the patches together, ½" (13mm) in from the edges. Turn the joined piece over and trim excess overlaps to ½" (13mm). Now, pin the insert to the skirt's opening, with a 1" (2.5cm) allowance all around. The patchwork can overlap the denim or be underlaid, whichever you think looks more groovy! Baste, remove the pins, and machine stitch ½" (13mm) from the edge. Repeat this process for the skirt back. If the top point of the insert join looks awkward, cover it with a patch.

3. **Tuck the Skirt:** Try the skirt on and pin tuck to snugly shape it around the lower hips and thighs. My project needed seven 2" (5cm) long tucks, stitched 11" (28cm) below the waist. Machine wash and dry. Press.

4. Make the Faux Petticoat Ruffle: Cut the georgette into 3 lengths, each measuring 5" (12.5cm) wide x 45" (114cm) long (or the width of your fabric). Using blush silk thread, finish all the edges with a machine zigzag stitch. Pin two lengths to form a long strip and stitch together with a ⅝" (15mm) seam allowance. Add the third length in the same way. Now sew the two ends together to form a tube. Press the seams open. Attach the lace to one edge, stitching ½" (13mm) above the edge of the silk with a machine zigzag stitch and blush thread. Stitch the other end of the long piece with a machine basting stitch. Pull one of the basting threads gently to form soft, even gathers. Pin the gathered edge of the ruffle to the lower edge of the skirt, with the denim overlapping the ruffle by 2" (5cm). Machine stitch ruffle to skirt 1½" (3.8cm) above the skirt edge, easing the gathers evenly all around. Baste and remove the pins. With ochre thread in the bobbin, blush thread for the top spool, and the silk on top, stitch ½" (13mm) from the lower edge of the silk. Repeat with a second ruffle, but this time make it 6½" (16.5cm) wide and sew it ½" (13mm) above the sewing line of the previous ruffle.

Be careful to avoid having a ruffle side seam at the center front or back. Keep the seams on the sides.

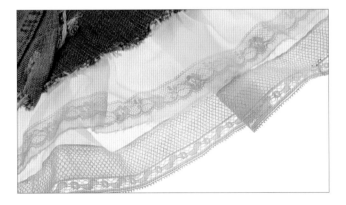

teddy bear tuxedo shirt

YOUR CHALLENGE

For this project you will re-craft a large-sized men's vintage tuxedo shirt with denim-trimmed funky DR attitude. Patches of stylish faded denim, pink gingham, and navy Western bandanas mix with playful, extra-large vintage buttons to create a colorful teddy bear sweetness. Use your craft-nik know-how to make this shirt to layer over denim shorts, leggings, or bathing suits.

teddy bear tuxedo shirt

teddy bear tuxedo shirt

How Difficult?

Intermediate. This project requires some basic sewing skills. Everyone's white cotton shirt will be different, so a bit of sewing experience is needed to adapt it to the shirt you're using as your base. Allow half a day to make it. Enjoy the project, because the cool combination of textures will camouflage any flaws in your technique.

What Denim Do I Need?

Soft, faded, and washed 100 percent cotton denim—enough for 2 sleeve cuffs and 1 front pocket (see patterns on pages 120 and 121).

What Other Materials Will I Need?

Your "Sewing Basket" (page 11)

20" (50cm) square cotton bandana kerchief in indigo and white, well washed

Photocopy of Cuff pattern (page 121)

Sewing machine

Denim blue, white, and ochre thread

Photocopy of Breast Pocket pattern (page 120)

Vintage (or oversized) tuxedo shirt

Denim blue embroidery floss

4½" diameter 2 hole buttons for cufflinks, or the size that will fit the buttonholes on your tuxedo shirt

7 1–1½" (2.5–3.8cm) assorted amusing, oversized novelty buttons

1 yard (1m) of pink cotton gingham

12" (30.5cm) of 1" (2.5cm) wide turquoise gingham ribbon, or the length of your front placket plus 1" (2.5cm)

2 toothpicks

HOW TO DO IT STEP BY STEP

1. **Make the Cuffs:** Using the Cuff pattern on page 121, cut 2 cuffs from the denim and 2 more from the bandana. Pin 1 denim cuff to 1 bandana cuff with wrong sides together. Baste, remove the pins, and machine-sew all around the perimeter with denim thread, ½" (13mm) from the edge. Repeat with the remaining 2 pieces, so you have two cuffs.

2. **Make the Pocket:** Using the Pocket pattern on page 120, cut 1 pocket piece from denim.

3. **Machine wash**, dry, and press the pocket and the two cuffs.

4. **Attach the Cuffs:** Pin 1 denim cuff around the right shirt cuff. Align it so that the denim faces up and it sits about 1" (2.5cm) above the shirt cuff seam. As you pin it, fold back the excess denim, as shown in the photo (on my project, the cuff folds back about 2½" (6.5cm)). With the embroidery floss, secure the cuff in place with 3 evenly spaced buttons. Remove the pins. Repeat with the other cuff on the left sleeve, but this time pin with the bandana material facing up.

5. **Make the Cufflinks:** Leaving a short thread end, sew 2 small buttons together into cufflinks with the denim embroidery floss. Sew back and forth 3 times with the toothpicks wedged between the buttons to serve as spacers. Remove the toothpicks and sew a few buttonhole stitches around the threads between the 2 buttons so the spacing is stabilized. Cut thread and securely knot the two thread ends together.

6. **Attach the Breast Pocket:** Cut a 1½"-wide x 4"-long (3.8cm x 10cm) strip of pink gingham on the bias. Fold it in half and pin it behind the top of the denim pocket, with the fold extending ¼" (6mm) above the edge. Baste, remove the pins, and machine-sew with ochre thread, ½" (13mm) from denim edge. Pin to the right chest of the shirt, baste, remove the pins, and machine-sew around the sides and bottom of the pocket, ½" (13mm) in from the edge.

7. **Jazz Up the Front Placket and Collar:** Line the front placket with the turquoise gingham ribbon. Pin it on the inside of the left placket, baste, and remove pins. With white thread in the bobbin and ochre in the top spool, machine zigzag stitch around the perimeter of the ribbon with ochre thread on the ribbon. Press. Sew the remaining oversized button to the right front collar.

8. **Trim the Back Shirt Tail:** Cut a length on the bias, 3" (7.5cm) wide, from pink gingham to match the width of the your back shirt tail. Pin the strip to the lower edge of the shirt tail with the shirt edge overlapping the gingham by ⅝" (15mm). Baste and remove the pins. Thread the machine with ochre thread in the top spool and white thread in the bobbin. Machine-stitch down the center of the overlap with the ochre thread on the white shirt. Leave the gingham edges raw. Press.

YOUR CHALLENGE

This retro skirt, outfitted with a
recycled scarf, is an alluring,
youthful style. It's about mixing
a classic scarf with the
nonchalant cool of worn jeans.
For this challenge, you will
convert a pair of jeans into a
jean skirt. You'll insert a scarf in
the skirt's V-shaped front and
back gaps to create a flirty,
fishtail shape. The first steps
will be hunting for a fabulous
scarf, patterned with colors
that you love, and choosing
the right jeans to remake. Scarf
It! is a great way to recycle
jeans that have a leg shape
that no longer works for you.
So happy hunting!

scarf it! skirt

scarf it! skirt

How Difficult?

Easy, skillwise, but allow half a day to complete the project because it takes a couple of hours to rip out all the inseams of the jeans and convert the pants into a skirt. Ripping out is brainless, so chat with some pals while you work and watch their amazement at your DR know-how!

What Denim Do I Need?

A pair of jeans that fits the way you like around the bum. Use a pair that has been washed and stressed to give the skirt a funkier character, more modern than vintage '60s. I used Clockhouse jeans in 100 percent cotton, fadeout, size 8.

What Other Materials Will I Need?

Your "Sewing Basket" (page 11)

Vintage silk scarf (the scarf I used was 30" (76cm) square, but the size is flexible)

Sewing machine

Thread to match the topstitching on your jeans

In most cases a standard sized square scarf will be sufficient to fill the v-shaped gap from extra small to extra large in a thigh- to mid-calf-length, but . . . if you want a much longer skirt, or your scarf is very small, or you are very tall, you can fill in the gap with more than one scarf, or you can use one scarf for the front opening and another for the back opening. It's DR pattern making!

HOW TO DO IT STEP BY STEP

1. **Reshape Your Jeans:** Decide the final skirt length you want (mine, a size Medium measures 26" (66cm) long) from the waistline to the hem). Mark the length with tailor's chalk and cut your jeans. Then follow the directions in the first paragraph of Convert a Pair of Jeans into a Denim Skirt on page 117. You will be left with long front and back V-shaped openings. Machine wash, dry, and press.

2. **Prepare the Scarf Insert:** Gently fold your scarf diagonally and press. Then open it up and cut along the fold line. Gently machine zigzag stitch along the cut edges as the diagonal on a silk scarf is stretchy and you don't want to pull the scarf out of shape. Press.

3. **Insert the Scarf:** Pin the center of the zigzagged edge of one of the scarf triangles to the center join point from the point to the hem. The denim should overlap the scarf by ¾" (2cm). Baste, remove the pins, and topstitch in place, imitating the edge-stitching style of the jeans. For example, if your jeans have a double row of stitching, then do that, or if there is a single row, then stitch that, just try to reflect the look of the jeans in your stitching and thread choice. Remove the basting. Repeat on the skirt back with the other piece of silk.

You now have a fabulous skirt made partly from an expensive silk scarf. I dry clean my skirt, but decide what works for you. You can also hand wash it in cold water or by machine on a gentle cycle. A good-quality silk will fade and soften over time, whereas an inexpensive one can just run—either can look fabulous!

YOUR CHALLENGE

Renew and re-energize by using your hands and imagination to "re-accessorize" and update a pair of jeans. For this challenge, take an old pair of jeans and reinvent them with stenciled flowers to give an individual, one-of-a-kind DR look.

flower-stamped basics

flower-stamped basics

How Difficult?

Beginner. Takes 15 minutes. If you have never stenciled before, check out Paint Stuff on page 114 and experiment. Play with the paints, stencils, and techniques on paper and denim scraps.

What Denim Do I Need?

A pair of jeans that you want to update and refresh. I used Bobby Anne, Spade Pocket 100 percent cotton. They're rugged, with rips and ink stains, and it all works with the pretty stenciled flowers.

What Other Materials Will I Need?

Newsprint

Masking tape

Floral stencil (Craft shops have many gorgeous floral stencils, mainly intended for home decoration that will adapt beautifully for clothes.)

Stencil sponges

Rag

Plate for mixing colors—any simple, old china or glass plate will work

Red, green, copper, and black fabric paint

HOW TO DO IT STEP BY STEP

1. **Prepare the Work Table:** Spread the newsprint on a table to protect it.

Read through Paint Stuff, page 114 for stenciling tips and techniques. Before you stencil your jeans, you may want to do as I did, and test your color choices by stenciling some denim scraps. The tests can be tossed into your I-box to use for future projects.

2. **Stencil Your Jeans:** Put the jeans on and hold the stencil up to decide where you want it. Mark the placement. Lay the jeans on the table and tape the stencil firmly in place. Squirt some of the different shades of paint on your plate. With the sponges, fill the flowers in with red paint, the leaves with green, and accent the flowers with copper and black paint. Mix your colors to add depth to the effect. For example, add some copper with red to get orange, or black with green to get olive. Let the paint dry, usually about 15–30 minutes, before removing the stencil. Machine wash, dry, and press.

YOUR CHALLENGE

Bring twenty-first-century attitude to a soft, pale blue denim skirt, transforming it with the sumptuous confections of eighteenth-century French court fashion. It's a combo of soft denim adorned with lilac taffeta, yards of ecru cotton lace, covered buttons, tucks, pleats, and pretty embroidery floss. The quality of the trims and your handcrafting is what makes it designer. Parisian Pouf is not for the faint of heart. It takes perseverance, but the rewards are big. With this project, you will create a family heirloom.

parisian pouf miniskirt

parisian pouf miniskirt

How Difficult?

Experienced. If you do the whole project the way I present it, hand-sewing experience is necessary, and you should love to hand-sew because there are lots of designer finishing touches top to bottom. It is a labor of love to sew on those gorgeous trims. It takes a weekend to finish this project.

What Denim Do I Need?

An old, faded pair of jeans. I used Poker-brand jeans, size 32/46. Key is that the jeans are faded so that they won't discolor the trims and the fit is slim on your waist and hips.

What Other Materials Will I Need?

Your "Sewing Basket" (page 11)

Photocopy of Godet pattern (page 120)

Pale gray embroidery floss

14 yards (15.5m) of 1" (2.5cm) wide 90% cotton/10% nylon ecru lace trim

3 lace appliqués to fit on the back pockets and yoke

3 yards (3.5m) of 3" (7.5cm) wide pale lilac silk taffeta ribbon

12 ¼" (2cm) diameter shank fabric-covered button forms in metal or plastic

Ecru thread

1½ yards (1.5m) ⅝" (15mm) wide dusty blush velvet ribbon

HOW TO DO IT STEP BY STEP

1. **Convert the Jeans:** Reshape your jeans into a skirt following the instructions in the first paragraph of Convert a Pair of Jeans into a Denim Skirt, page 117).

2. **Cut the Skirt to Length:** Lay your skirt flat and use tailor's chalk to mark the lower edge cutting line, referring to **diagram 1.** After you have marked the line, try the skirt on and make adjustments to match your body shape or preferred length. If you make adjustments to the length, apply your change to the Godet pattern in step 4, making it smaller or larger as needed. Lay the skirt flat and cut the length.

diagram 1

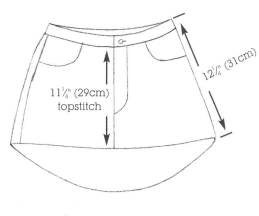

11¼" (29cm) topstitch

12¼" (31cm)

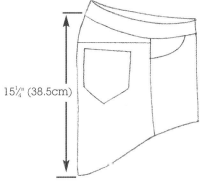

15¼" (38.5cm)

3. Remove the Waist Details: With a seam ripper, carefully remove all belt loops and the back waistband label.

4. Make the Back Skirt Godets: Using the Godet pattern on page 120, cut 3 denim pieces on the bias. Following **diagram 2,** pin the 3 godets to the skirt back, allowing a 1" (2.5cm) fold of ease in the godet at the hem.

Try the skirt on to check that the curve of your hemline is pretty and smooth. If you need to make any adjustments, now is the time to redraw the line and cut.

Baste the godets in place, remove the pins, and whip-stitch all around the godets with pale gray embroidery floss. Remove the basting. Trim inside the seam allowance on the wrong side of the godets to ½" (13mm), and overcast the raw edges with the embroidery floss. Using a pressing cloth, press the godet seams on the inside.

5. Add the Lace Edging: Apply the 1" (2.5cm) wide lace with small pintuck pleats, about ⅜" (1cm) deep and ¾" (2cm) apart.

Following **diagram 3,** pin a line of pleated lace down the left side front of the skirt. Baste and remove the pins. Sew in place with embroidery floss and running stitch, ⅛" (3mm) from the lace edge. Remove the basting. Repeat on the right side front and left and right back sides. Repeat along the hem, overlapping the skirt hem by ¼" (6mm). Add 2 more rows of lace along the hem. Each layer of lace should overlap the lower one by ¼" (6mm). Sew these 2 rows of lace flat, only adding ⅜" (1cm) tucks as necessary to follow the curve around the back hem so the outer lace edge will lie smooth.

diagram 2

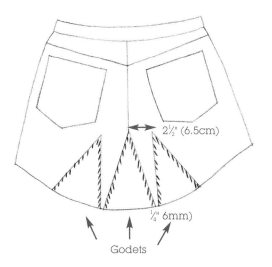

2½" (6.5cm)

¼" 6mm)

Godets

You don't need to make these pleats with mechanical regularity. Any imprecision in the pleating and the hand embroidery can be charming, so whatever your sewing ability, enjoy working with the fine lace stitch by stitch.

diagram 3

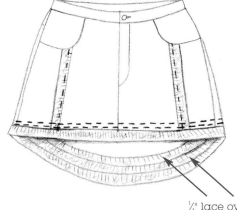

¼" lace overlap

6. Sow on Back Lace Appliqués: Pin individual appliqués on the back pockets and back yoke. See photograph as a guide and balance your pieces depending on their size and shape. Baste. Remove the pins and sew with embroidery floss. Remove the basting.

7. Make Taffeta Ruffles: Cut 24" (61cm) each of the taffeta ribbon and the lace trim. With running stitch and embroidery floss, hand-sew the lace to one edge of the taffeta, with the taffeta ribbon overlapping the lace trim by ⅛" (3mm). Following **diagram 4,** pin the taffeta to the skirt, starting on the left front, about ⅛" (6mm) from the zipper (allow just enough space so that it won't get caught in the zipper teeth). Double fold back the raw edge of the taffeta ribbon and pin it along the edge of the center front waistband; continue following the edge of the front pocket, ending at the side seam. The shape you are following is a curve, so you need to tuck the taffeta to follow this shape. I needed 8 tucks, ⅜" (1cm) deep, to form the shape. At the side seam, fold the excess material into a box pleat. Baste, remove the pins, and sew with embroidery floss and whipstitch. Remove the basting. Repeat on the right front, but cut the length of the taffeta and lace 1" (2.5cm) longer to allow for the center front zipper extension.

The appliqués I found were actually intended for a collar. Search for something special that you love; there are plenty of beautiful laces available, and this is a modern way to use them.

diagram 4

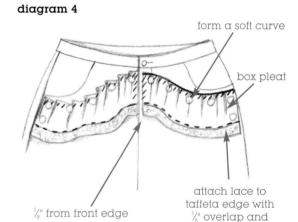

form a soft curve

box pleat

⅛" from front edge

attach lace to taffeta edge with ⅛" overlap and running stitch

8. Add the Buttons: Cover the buttons with the taffeta following product instructions. Some covered buttons need to be hand stitched; others will snap in place. I find it is best to not be lazy and gather the silk around the shank with a few stitches regardless. Once all the buttons are covered, sew 4 of them evenly spaced along the upper edge of the front ruffle, and 2 at each side, as shown in the photograph below. The buttons are for decorative purposes only, but sew them on securely.

9. Jazz Up the Back Inside Waistband: Cut 21" (53.5cm) lengths each of taffeta ribbon and lace trim. As in step 7, sew the lace to one edge of the taffeta. Following **diagram 5,** fold a box pleat ⅝" (15mm) deep in the center. Then fold 4 pleats on each side, spaced ⅝" (15mm) apart and ⅝" (15mm) deep; ⅝" (15mm) from the last tuck, double fold the balance of the ribbon. Pin to the center back waist, centered horizontally and rising 2" (5cm) above the top of the waistband at the center back. Baste and remove the pins.

10. Finish the Inside Waist: Pin lace trim around the inside of the waistband, folding the raw lace edge back ⅝" (15mm) at each front edge and aligning the top edge of the lace just below the top of the waistband. Baste and remove the pins. With ecru thread, sew the lace in place with a running stitch, being careful to catch only the wrong side of the waistband.

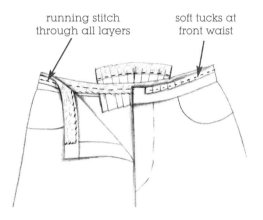

running stitch through all layers — soft tucks at front waist

diagram 5

11. Sew on the Velvet Ribbon: Pin the velvet ribbon around the outside of the waistband, aligning the top edge of the ribbon with the top stitch line of the waistband. Beginning 1¼" (3cm) from the right front waistband edge, fold the ribbon under ⅝" (15mm), then pin 6 pleats, ¼" (6mm) deep and ¾" (2cm) apart. Now pin the ribbon flat until you come to the left front of the skirt; repeat the 6 pleats in the same way as for the right front. Baste and remove the pins. Sew a running stitch with embroidery floss in the center of the ribbon, catching the lace facing, the taffeta ribbon at the center back, and the velvet.

This is a delicately embellished piece, so hand wash and line dry or dry clean.

simply lovely

Fairy tales, romantic evenings, and parties at their most hip require eye-catching looks. These designs are made for glamorous holiday adventures, intimate gatherings, and just for fun. Their flirty, whimsical style is impossible to resist.

YOUR CHALLENGE

Watch out—these gauntlets are so appealing that once you make them, you'll wear them all the time! You will pin and cut out the pattern, sew up the gauntlets, and contrast the rugged denim with luxurious trims like an extravagant beaded braid that drips around your fingers and a lime silk taffeta accent. It's hip glamour—twenty-first century romance!

pretty woman gauntlets

pretty woman gauntlets

pretty woman gauntlets

How Difficult?

Easy. You need a bit of sewing experience. It takes a half day to complete. This project is a little jewel of a craft to work on, and friends will be transfixed by your awesome design and craft ability. If you want a Beginner project, skip the embellishment and just go for the raw denim look.

What Denim Do I Need?

Sturdy, 100 percent cotton basic denim, in a medium washed shade. You will need enough denim to cut 4 pieces from the Gauntlet pattern (page 121).

What Other Materials Will I Need?

Your "Sewing Basket" (page 11)

Photocopy of Gauntlet pattern (page 121)

Sewing machine

Denim blue thread

1½ yards (1½m) of 1" (2.5cm) white and pearl beaded braid

Denim blue embroidery floss

1 yard (1m) of 3" (7.5cm) wide iridescent lime/blue silk taffeta ribbon

HOW TO DO IT STEP BY STEP

1. **Cut the Denim:** Cut out 2 denim pieces from the Gauntlet pattern. Then flip the pattern over and cut out 2 more pieces. Machine wash, dry, and press.

Let's talk fit and sizing! This style does not need to fit like a glove, it just needs to fit comfortably. Pin one of the denim gauntlets together along the seam leaving the slit opening. Slip it on, with the seam allowance on the outside. Do you like how it feels and looks? If it's a bit snug or too loose, then see if reducing or increasing the slit opening a bit will solve the problem. If that doesn't work then slip it off, and adjust the size by pinning the seam allowance a bit larger or smaller. Slip it on again. Does that work? It probably will for S-M-L, but if you are size XS or XL, you may need to adjust the pattern by enlarging or reducing the pattern ¼" (6mm) in width and ⅜" (1cm) in length. Check out Pattern Adjustments on page 12.

2. **Sew the Denim:** Sew seams with denim blue thread as marked on the pattern. Clip the seams as marked on the pattern and press open. Hey beginners—it's finished! Enjoy—or continue to add embellishments, below.

3. **Add the Beads:** Pin the bead trim around the cuff opening and side slit with the denim overlapping the trim. Baste, remove the pins, and sew with embroidery floss in a running stitch. Remove the basting.

4. Attach the Taffeta Lining: Turn one of the gauntlets inside out. Pin the taffeta ribbon all around the top opening of the gauntlet, wrong sides together. Place the joining of the ribbon ends at the gauntlet seam with a ⅝" (1.5cm) seam allowance. Baste and remove the pins. Stitch with embroidery floss and a running stitch ¼" (6mm) from the ribbon edge. Whipstitch the ribbon joining and tack it in a couple of places on the side seam. Repeat on the other gauntlet.

YOUR CHALLENGE

Recycle those boring, basic
jeans into romantic trousers
with loose, generous legs. To
achieve the look, you will
insert wide, box-pleated
panels of plush red cotton
velvet and tack them with rich
gold braid and velvet bows.
These wide-legged pants are
the hip way to go—make
them yours!

harlequin trousers

harlequin trousers

How Difficult?

Intermediate. This project takes a few hours to do right. You will do some hand- and machine-sewing, and because velvet has a pile, some experience is needed.

What Denim Do I Need?

A pair of jeans with straight, loose legs. I used AG Adirano Goldschmied, W32 L32, 100 percent cotton, medium-faded with red topstitching, and a 19" (48.5cm) cuff opening.

What Other Materials Will I Need?

Your "Sewing Basket" (page 11)

Sewing machine

Denim blue thread

½ yard (.5m) red cotton velvet (if you cut it cross-grain as I did, this amount is enough, otherwise you will need a piece to match your pant length. See my explanation in the pattern.)

1 yard (1m) of 1" (2.5cm) wide metallic openwork ribbon

1 yard (1m) of 1" (2.5cm) wide red velvet ribbon

Red embroidery floss

2 brass buckles, ⅝" x 1⅜" (15mm x 3.5cm)

HOW TO DO IT STEP BY STEP

I committed a couple of faux-pas in the cutting that I love, but they're not traditional sewing techniques so I want to explain them. I used the velvet selvage at the jean hem. Generally selvages are cut off and not used as an edge finish, but I find it funky with recycled jeans. So in step 2, the velvet panels are cut with the 7" (18cm) width at the selvage. Therefore the velvet is cut across the grain instead of along the length of the fabric. Fabric drapes better when cut along the length, but I like the look of seeing the selvage at the hem—it's a designer prerogative, deciding which rules to break. Whatever you do, keep the pile in the same direction on both legs.

1. **Cut the Jeans:** Lay your jeans flat, folded with front and back creases and inseams matched up (as men's slacks are hung on a hanger). Mark the front crease line with tailor's chalk. Open the jeans and lay them flat, front side up. Following **diagram 1,** draw a straight line with tailor's chalk and a yardstick, matching up your chalk marks, from the hem to 2" (5cm) below the pocket

diagram 1

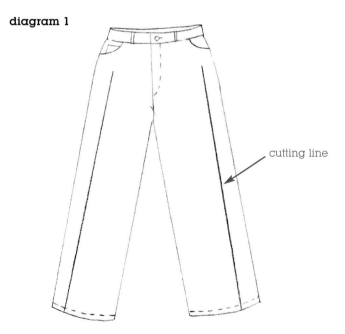

cutting line

opening. Try the jeans on and check that the chalk line falls nice and straight. Take them off, lay them flat again, and cut along the line. Using denim blue thread, machine zigzag stitch around the cut edges.

2. Make the Velvet Inserts: Cut the velvet fabric into two strips, 7" (18cm) wide (at the selvage) and the length of your jean cutting line plus 1" (2.5cm). I used a 36" (91cm) length. Machine zigzag stitch all around the velvet cut edges. Following **diagram 2,** pin the velvet to the jeans with right sides together from the cuff to 1" (2.5cm) before the top of the opening. Baste, remove the pins, and machine-sew the velvet with a ⅝" (15mm) seam allowance. Using a pressing cloth, steam the seams open on the wrong side, lightly steaming the denim, never the velvet!

Velvet is plush, and it can slip on the sewing machine, so don't skip the basting, and sew slowly to get a nice, even join line.

3. Pleat the Velvet: Following **diagram 3,** pull the excess velvet through to the wrong side of the jeans. Fold the velvet into a ½" (13mm) double box pleat at the top of the opening. With the denim thread, hand-sew the pleats securely to the denim.

4. Make the Bows: Cut the metallic and red velvet ribbons each into 14" (35.5cm) lengths. Lay the metallic one over the red velvet ribbon and hand-sew them neatly together around the perimeter with red embroidery floss and running stitch. Slip the ribbon through the buckle and, following **diagram 4,** gracefully fold each ribbon into a decorative bow. With red embroidery floss hand tack the bow and the buckle at the top of the velvet inserts, covering the top of the cut line.

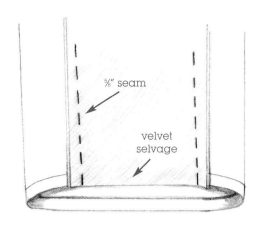

Back side

⅝" seam

velvet selvage

diagram 2

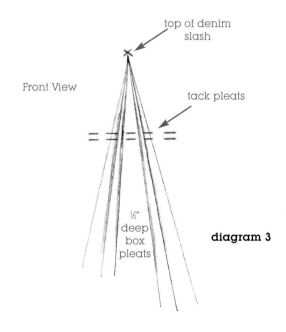

Front View

top of denim slash

tack pleats

½" deep box pleats

diagram 3

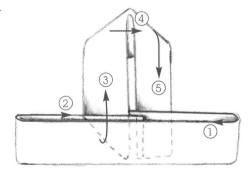

diagram 4

glitzy poet beret

YOUR CHALLENGE

Create an eye-catchingly ornate beret. The cap base is formed from a simple circle of faded denim that you will embellish with golden braids and buttons. The contrast of denim with ornate is modern and whimsical. Making this project offers a whole lot of crafting fun.

glitzy poet beret

glitzy poet beret

How Difficult?

Intermediate. Some sewing experience is necessary to align the ribbons straight and sew the crown together. Allow 2 to 3 hours to complete this challenge.

What Denim Do I Need?

A piece of washed and worn denim large enough to cut a 16" (40.5cm) diameter circle for the cap and a 1½" x 30" (3.8cm x 76cm) strip for the hatband.

What Other Materials Will I Need?

Your "Sewing Basket" (page 11)

19" (48.5cm) of ⅛" (3mm) wide gold silk cord

2 yards (2m) piece of ½" (13mm) wide olive cotton ribbon

19" (48.5cm) of ⅝" (15mm) wide ivy silk velvet ribbon

1 yard (1m) of ¼" (6mm) wide ruffled metallic braid

1 yard (1m) of 1" (2.5cm) wide metallic ribbon

Sewing machine

Gold silk thread

Pale lime embroidery floss

½ yard (.5m) denim blue lining fabric

1 yard (1m) of 1" (2.5cm) wide lime cotton grosgrain ribbon for the facing

8 gold buttons, ¾" (2cm) diameter

7 gold buttons, ⅝" (15mm) diameter

You need an assortment of at least 5 different ribbons to make it lush. I focused on golds and greens to create this group of ribbons. Some of mine are vintage and some are new. Use my assortment as a guide and do it your way, in your favorite color, with what you have or find!

HOW TO DO IT STEP BY STEP

1. **Mark the Cap:** Mark the center of your circle with tailor's chalk. Mark 16 evenly spaced points around the circumference.

2. **Play with the Ribbons:** Lay the ribbons and braids (not including the grosgrain ribbon for the facing) across the circle, from point to opposite point around the circumference. Stand back and look at your layout. Do you like it? If not, play with the placement until you are happy with the look.

3. **Attach the Ribbons:** Trim the ribbons and braids even with the edge of the circle's diameter. Set them to the side carefully so you know which goes where. Pull the bottom ribbon from the pile and lay it in position on the denim, pin, baste, remove the pins, and sew to the cap. Repeat for the other ribbons and braids, overlapping them at the center point.

I machine-sewed the ⅛" (3mm) wide gold braid and the ¼" (6mm) wide metallic ruffled ribbon to the denim with gold silk thread and a zigzag stitch. I hand-sewed the 1" (2.5cm) wide metallic braid along the edges. The other ribbons were hand-sewn with lime embroidery floss and a running stitch, down the center.

4. **Sew the Lining:** Cut out a 16" (40.5cm) diameter circle from the lining material. With wrong sides together, lay the lining on the cap and pin together around the edge. Baste and remove the pins. With the silk thread, machine-sew the 2 layers together, ⅜" (1cm) from the edge. Remove the basting.

5. Add Tucks around the Crown: Pin ½" (13mm) deep tucks around the edge of the circle, spacing one tuck at the edge of each ribbon.

Try on the hat to check the fit. If you want it snugger, increase the depth of the tucks. If you want it looser, reduce the depth of the tucks.

When your hat fits the way you like it, baste the tucks in place and remove the pins.

6. Assemble the Hatband: Pin the grosgrain ribbon to the inside of the cap, aligned with the outer edge. Baste and remove the pins. Cover the cap edge with the denim strip, folding it with ½" (13mm) in front and the rest in the back. Cut any excess denim length, making a neat join with a 1" (2.5cm) overlap. Baste and remove the pins. Hand-sew with embroidery floss and running stitch, ¼" (6mm) from the front denim edge, all around the denim band, stitching through all the layers.

7. Decorate with the Buttons: Sew a large button at the top center of the cap. Sew the remaining buttons around the cap band, evenly spaced and alternating the sizes.

I love to create textures, so I layered the metallic braid over the olive cotton ribbon and gave the olive cotton ribbon ¼" (6mm) tucks about ½" (13mm) apart. I also adore the ruffled metallic braid and the metallic braid overlaid on the olive cotton ribbon so much that I used each of these versions twice in the cap. Experiment and express yourself!

Your ribbons should be sewn straight and the overlapped center point should be neat and perfect. It's helpful to sew each ribbon from the center point to the outer edge.

YOUR CHALLENGE

Recycle denim scraps into a romantically chic capelet. The pearly white beads that are sewn along the edge cast an eccentric loveliness against the dark fur collar and old, worn denim. Accept the challenge, and this fabulously dreamy mini-cloak will be yours to wear dressed up or down, day or evening. But prepare yourself: Friends will plead with you to make them one!

russian cloak

russian cloak

How Difficult?

Intermediate. You need a bit of sewing experience and about a day to complete the project. Take time to find the wonderful elements that make it cool—the brown fur collar, the old fashioned leather button, and pearl beaded edging. If you love beading, create your own, unique bead trim!

What Denim Do I Need?

A variety of large denim scraps from different well-worn jeans. The worn and faded effect is key to the style and looks pretty with the trims. All the denim that I used was 100 percent basic cotton.

What Other Materials Will I Need?

Your "Sewing Basket" (page 11)

Photocopy of Cloak patterns (page 123)

Sewing machine

Denim blue thread

3½" x 16" (9cm x 40.5cm) piece of faux mink or real fur

Chocolate and denim blue embroidery floss

3 yards (3m) of 1" (2.5cm) wide beaded braid

1" (2.5cm) diameter honey-colored leather shank button

HOW TO DO IT STEP BY STEP

1. **Cut the Denim:** Dump your I-box on a table and pull out the larger pieces. Press them and lay them flat. Place the Cloak patterns on the denim pieces to decide which scrap of denim works best for each pattern piece. Balance the different shades and seams of the denim.

The pattern is in a size Medium. If necessary, size the pattern larger or smaller. Don't stress—you can't go wrong with denim! I would suggest to grade 1" (2.5cm) for every size, generalizing the sizes as XS-S-M-L-XL. Follow the information on Sizing and Pattern Adjustments on page 12. Recycled denim is a great material on which to hone your pattern-making skills. Any mistakes can be recycled into other projects, and the fabric is not slippery or difficult to work with. This heavy duty fabric helps you along and is very forgiving!

Once you are content with the balance and variety of denim, pin the patterns and cut out the pieces. You need both a right and left front and back, so cut each piece once with the right side up and once with the it flipped over. Cut an additional 3½" x 16" (9cm x 40.5cm) piece of denim for the undercollar. Machine wash, dry, and press all the denim pieces.

2. **Assemble the Cloak:** Pin the cloak together along the shoulder line with the front overlapping the back, by 1" (2.5cm). Baste and remove the pins. With blue thread, machine topstitch down the center of the overlap. Repeat on the balance of the seams. Press.

3. **Sew the Collar**: Following **diagram 1,** with wrong sides of the fur and the denim strip together, whipstitch the collar together with chocolate embroidery floss. Start at the side, ¾" (2cm) from the bottom edge, continue up the side, around the top edge, and finally down the other side stopping ¾" (2cm) from the bottom edge.

4. **Attach the Collar to the Cape**: Following **diagram 2,** pin the collar to the cape, with the cape sandwiched between the fur and denim of the collar. Align the center of the collar with the center back neck of the cape. Overlap the seam ⅝" (1.5cm). Compare and check that your front edge join points are the same measurement and then baste. Remove the pins and whipstitch the collar to the cape with chocolate embroidery floss, following **diagram 2.**

5. **Sew on the Beads**: Hand-sew the beaded braid around the edge of the cloak with denim embroidery floss in a running stitch, having the denim overlap the braid. Start at the top right front neck edge and work around to the top left neck edge. Be sure to hide the knotted thread ends well.

diagram 1

diagram 2

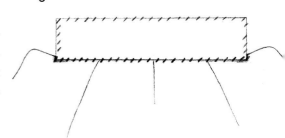

6. Add the Button and Loop: With blue embroidery floss sew the button on the left side at the top neck, just below the collar join point. Knot the thread securely, then neatly catch a few stitches to hide your thread ends inside the collar. For the right side, as shown in the photo, form a loop that will fit over your button with a double strand of blue embroidery floss. Sew the loop ends securely in place to correspond to the button. With doubled floss, sew blanket stitch all along the loop, working around the doubled strand. Knot off and hide the thread ends.

Dry clean only.

YOUR CHALLENGE

Create cuffs that Marie Antoinette would have envied! This project is all about romance and alluring denim style. You will take worn, old denim in a soft blue shade, cut out the cuff pattern, and trim it with delicate French ecru cotton lace, fine cotton gros-grain, and velvet ribbons in bluebell shades. All of it is accented with old-fashioned jet-black buttons. They're fun to make and a dream to wear.

victorian romance lacy cuffs

victorian romance lacy cuffs

How Difficult?

Intermediate. Sewing the trims on takes a little bit of skill. Allow a morning to do it.

What Denim Do I Need?

A piece of softly worn, 100 percent cotton basic denim on which you can fit 2 pieces of the pattern (page 122) on.

What Other Materials Will I Need?

Your "Sewing Basket" (page 11)
Photocopy of Victorian pattern (page 122)
4 yards (4m) of 1" (2.5cm) wide French lace trim in ecru
Sewing machine
Denim blue thread
2 yards (2m) of ⅛" (3mm) wide velvet ribbon in blue
1 yard (1m) of ¾" (2cm) wide cotton grosgrain ribbon in bluebell
8 jet-black shank buttons, ⅜" (1cm) diameter
¾" x 2" (2cm x 5cm) piece of iron-on Velcro

Let's talk sizing! On one of the denim cuffs, pin the box pleat as described in Step 4. Hold the cuff on your wrist with a ½" (13mm) overlap at the closure. Does it fit your wrist? If it's a bit snug or too loose, then adjust the depth of the box pleat. Check out Pattern Adjustments on page 12.

HOW TO DO IT STEP BY STEP

1. **Cut the Denim:** From denim, cut out 2 cuff pieces using the Victorian pattern on page 122. Machine wash, dry, and press.

2. **Attach the Lace:** Pin 2 yards (2m) of the lace trim into small tucks about ½" (13mm) apart and ¼" (6mm) deep all around the edge of one of the cuffs, with the denim overlapping the trim by ¼" (6mm). Baste, remove the pins, and machine topstitch the lace to the denim. Remove the basting. Repeat on the other cuff.

3. **Sew on the Velvet:** Pin and baste the velvet ribbon around the outside edge of the cuff, ¼" (6mm) from the edge. Remove the pins and machine zigzag stitch the ribbon to the denim. Remove the basting. Repeat on the other cuff.

4. **Pleat the Cuff:** At the center of the cuff, fold a 1¼" (3cm) wide box pleat. Pin and baste into place. Stitch the pleat securely by hand or machine.

5. **Make Grosgrain Bows:** With half of the grosgrain ribbon, form a bow, following the **diagram** (below, left). Hand-stitch the center of the bow, then sew it to the box pleat, covering the pleat stitching line. Repeat on the other cuff.

6. **Sew on the Buttons:** Sew 2 decorative buttons on the bow. Center 1 button on each side opening and sew in place.

7. **Make the Velcro Closure:** Cut the Velcro into two ⅜" x 2" (13mm x 5cm) strips. Following product instructions, adhere a closure to each cuff.

paint stuff

Tools: Paint brushes, fabric paint, stencils, spray paint, permanent markers, masking tape, scissors, computer printouts, bleach, newspaper, paper towels. Go into hardware stores or craft shops and ask what types of products they have to paint, dye, or bleach denim. Explore.

Painting on Denim

Use fabric paint! Fabric paint will retain the color through wear and tear and will not change the hand-feel or the texture of the denim. Read any special directions on the package. Before you paint your jeans, experiment on denim scraps. Test colors and techniques. Experiment with different techniques of application: Apply the paint with brushes or sponges; drip or smear it with a spatula. Machine wash, dry, and press your tests to check the results. Keep your test patches—they make wonderful scraps for future projects.

House Paint? Yeah! If you want a wildly crazy look, then do a Jackson Pollack by dripping some high-gloss house paint over your jeans. But use this paint very gingerly, as it will harden and change the feel of your jeans.

Spray Cans! Yes, fabric paint also comes in spray cans, which are great fun to use for stencils or just spraying all over. White and metallic shades are very cool.

Permanent Fabric Pens: Scribble notes and draw to your heart's delight. Yes, you are allowed to draw on your denim clothes!

Stenciling on Denim

Craft stores have a wonderful variety of stencils that are inexpensive and loads of fun. I suggest you buy a few and freely experiment. Follow the instructions on the packages, testing on denim scraps prior to stenciling your jeans. You can also test on paper, but the colors will look quite different on denim.

1. **Secure the stencil as flat as possible on the denim.** The easiest method is to tape it down with masking tape. You can also weight the stencil down with a heavy can, a stone, or hold it with one of your hands while you paint with the other. This way the stencil won't shift during the painting, paint won't seep under the stencil, and you'll get clean lines around the stencil edges.

2. **Dip a dry sponge in the paint,** then lightly pat it on a dry rag or newsprint to evenly distribute the paint on the sponge.

3. **Dab the area with an up and down movement where you want to put the color.** If you are using multiple colors, use separate sponges.

4. **Once the paint is dry,** peel off the stencil and admire your work!

Experiment—for example, if you dab on top of another color, you are also mixing colors, which will give a different effect and texture. Use different sizes of brushes and sponges for different effects. You can also spray-paint stencils.

Make your own stencils by drawing freehand, tracing over a drawing, or using a computer. When printing from a computer, I used regular paper, which works because I only use the stencils once or twice. If you have it available, use a nonabsorbent paper or heavyweight paper. It is great fun to create your own stencils, so try it!

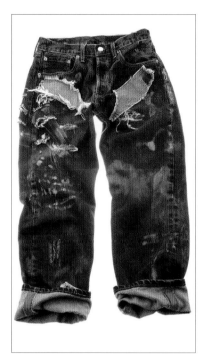

Bleaching Denim

Bleach gives another interesting effect. Do it in the bathtub, in the garden, or someplace where you will not damage anything else. Clean up well afterward— bleach is powerful stuff. Pour, sprinkle, or spray it on. Watch the process as it bleaches out the denim, and when you like the look, quickly stop it by washing the bleach out in the bathtub, with a hose in the garden, or in the sink. Just don't let the bleach drip anywhere else but on the jeans. Test it out on scraps first!

Add Wear-and-Tear to Your Jeans

Sandpaper: Put your jeans on, and mark with tailor's chalk the area you want to distress. Then slide a bulky, firm object, such as a thick book or a block of wood, into the pant leg under the chalk mark. Pull the denim tightly around it. With coarse sand paper, sand the denim. It's okay if the denim tucks up a bit—it adds texture. Stop occasionally to machine wash and dry, and check the development of your distressing. Continue until you are happy with the look.

Slashes: Put on your jeans and mark with tailor's chalk where you want rips. Take the jeans off,

cut the slashes, and machine wash and dry to see the effect. The cut lines can be little, long, on the bias, vertical, or horizontal.

Another slash effect is to put on your jeans and mark with tailor's chalk where you want a slash. Carefully cut the slash as long as you like but not all the way through. Cut along what is the cross grain, from the side seam to the inseam. With a seam ripper, gently pull the threads above and below your cut line to unravel them, exposing the horizontal white threads and unweaving the vertical indigo ones until you have the look you want. Machine wash and dry to check your work. Clip the indigo threads if you wish. If your slashes are quite large in stress points, such as at the knees, be aware that the white threads will eventually break, and you will soon have big holes. You will need to reinforce the slashes.

Reinforced Slash: After you have unraveled your slash line as described above, you can reinforce the slashes to retain the look and prevent the hole from expanding. Lay the jeans flat on an ironing board. Lay a piece of white iron-on patch about 2" (5cm) larger than the slash underneath it with the glue side up. Neatly smooth the stressed slash so that all the white cotton threads lie smooth and parallel on the patch. Press. Turn the jeans inside out and firmly steam the patch for a minute or two to adhere to the denim. You should see just a bit of the white patch showing through the threads. You could also reinforce and add texture by heavily machine zigzag stitching the iron-on patch. Or you could back the slash with a scrap of denim by sewing it on with hand-stitching all around. Or back it with a bright red fabric, stitch around the edge of the slash, and when the horizontal threads break, the red will peek out. Experiment. Play!

Nails: Take a big nail, a hammer, and a solid wooden block. Mark where you want holes, then slip the block into the jeans under the marked area. Hammer the nail repeatedly into the area, pulling it out each time and nailing into another place. When you machine wash and dry your jeans, they will have wonderful little textured holes wherever you nailed.

convert a pair of jeans into a denim skirt

Try the jeans on and mark your preferred skirt length. Lay the jeans flat, and with a yardstick and tailor's chalk, draw the new length, checking that the side seams are the same length. Then cut the jeans at least 2" (5cm) longer than the final skirt length. With a seam ripper, rip out the inseams from the cut line to the top of the inseam. In the front, continue ripping to an inch below the zipper; in the back, continue to 5" (12.5cm) below the waist. Machine wash, dry, and press all the seams that you just ripped out flat and open. Lay the jeans flat, front side up, and flatten out the skirt. You'll need to fiddle with it to get the nicest, most natural shape. Pin. Stitch the inseam closed following the style and thread of the topstitching on the jeans as closely as possible.

V-Shaped Insert: If your skirt will be longer than the new front and back length, lay a scrap of denim (or whatever fabric you want to use) underneath the gap, pinning with about a ¾" (2cm) overlap. Baste, then remove the pins. Turn the skirt over and repeat on the back. Try on the skirt to check the length and the look, and adjust if necessary.

Hem and Stitching: Now you need to decide how you want to finish the hem and add any extra length for the finish. With tailor's chalk, mark a neat line for the finished hem. Getting an even and straight hem is usually pretty easy on jean skirts because of their sturdy shape, but take the time to check the hem from all views to make sure it hangs evenly before you cut. Machine topstitch the front and back inseams and insert panels (if you added inserts), matching the color, type of thread, and stitch to the other seams on the jeans. Trim the seam allowance on the inside to ½" (13mm).

If your center join point is a bit lumpy, sew a patch on top of the problem area.

patterns & templates

The following templates will need to be photocopied and enlarged to the appropriate size before you pin them to your fabric. In small quantities, for personal use, you are free to make photocopies from this book.

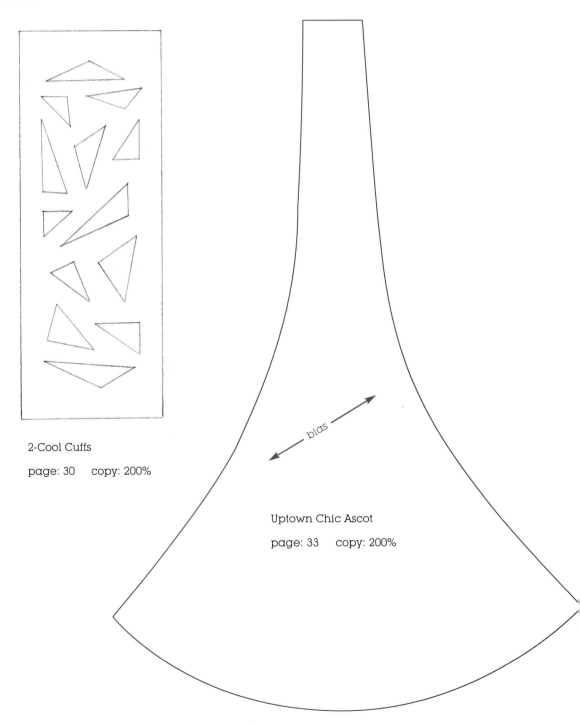

2-Cool Cuffs

page: 30   copy: 200%

Uptown Chic Ascot

page: 33   copy: 200%

Moth Holes Bite the Dust

page: 16   copy: 100%

Toreador Style Patches

page: 44   copy: 100%

Alice in Wonderland Pedal Pushers Heart

page: 62   copy: 100%

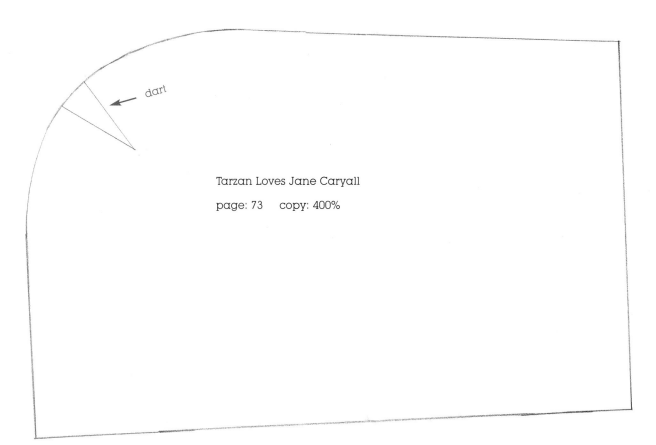

dart

Tarzan Loves Jane Caryall

page: 73   copy: 400%

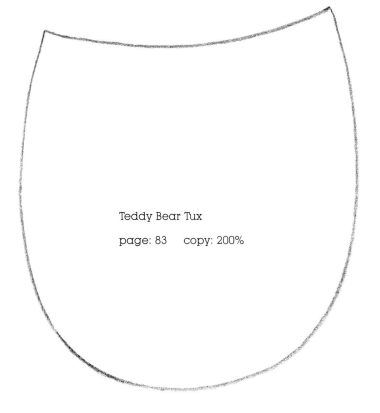

Teddy Bear Tux

page: 83   copy: 200%

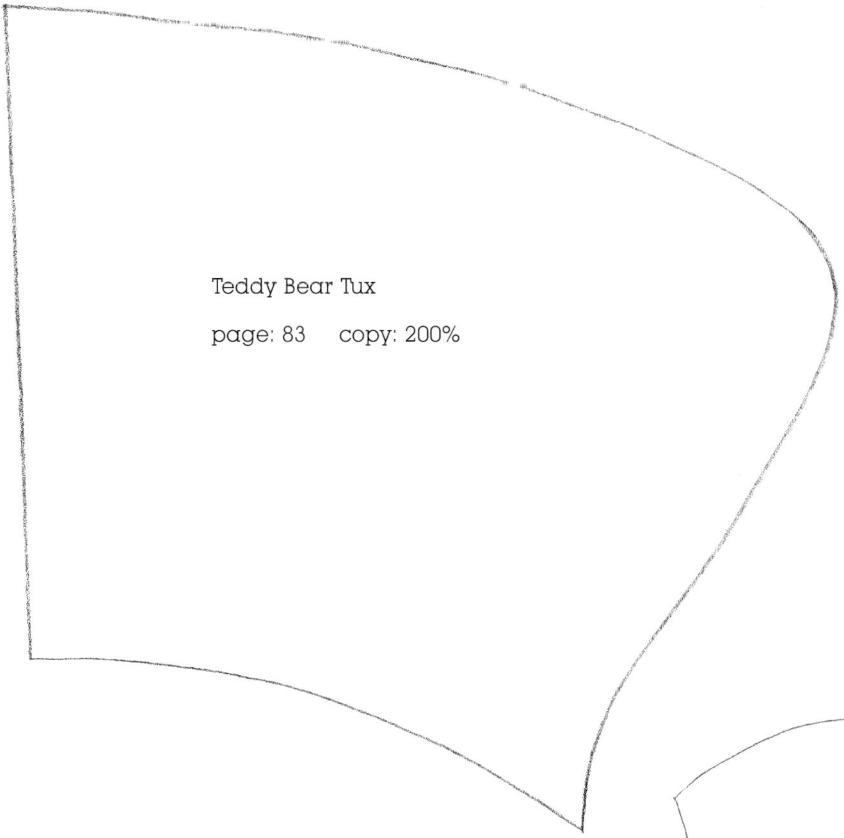

Teddy Bear Tux

page: 83   copy: 200%

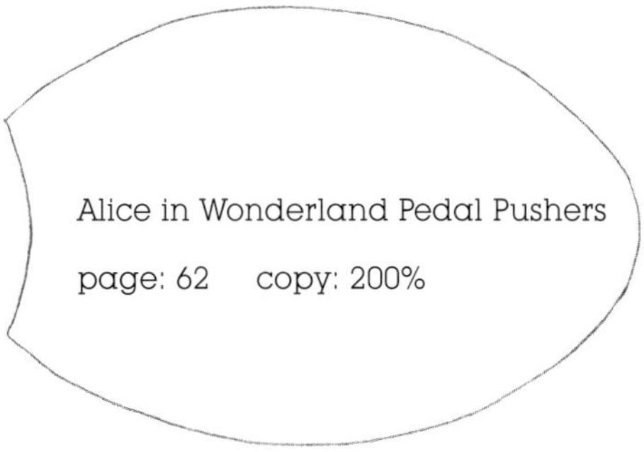

Alice in Wonderland Pedal Pushers

page: 62   copy: 200%

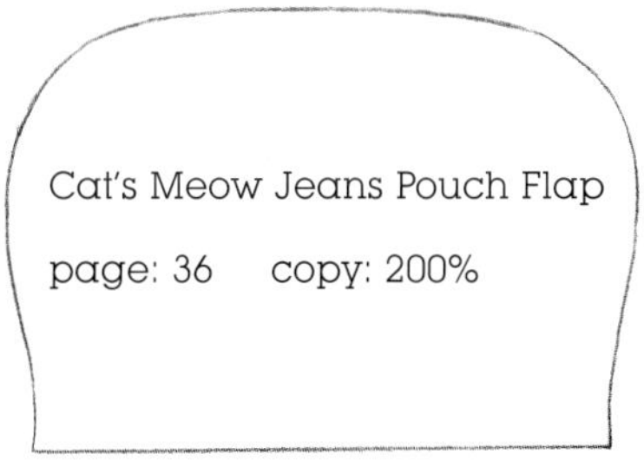

Cat's Meow Jeans Pouch Flap

page: 36   copy: 200%

Cat's Meow Jeans Pouch

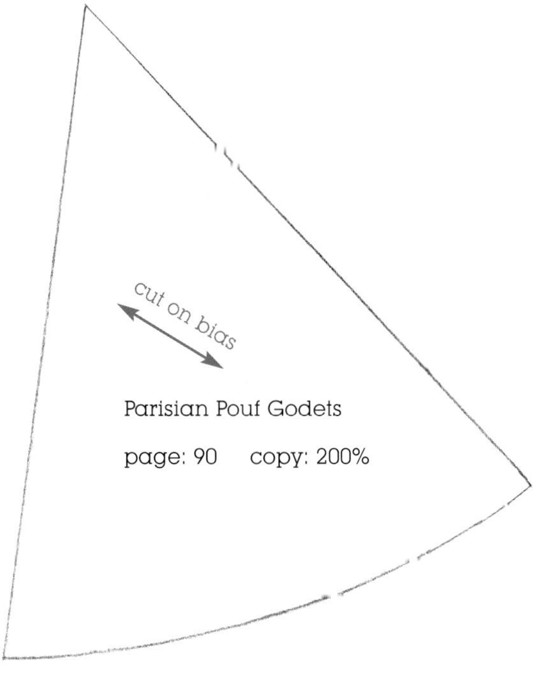

cut on bias

Parisian Pouf Godets

page: 90   copy: 200%

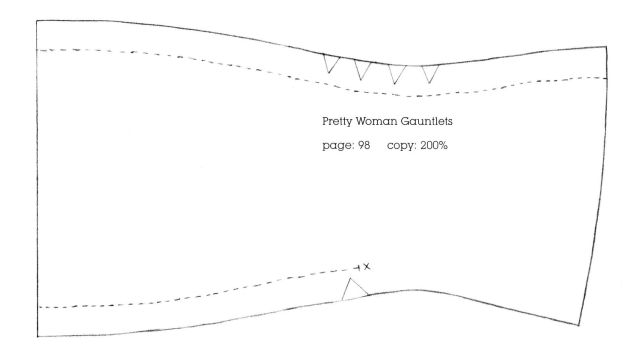

Pretty Woman Gauntlets

page: 98   copy: 200%

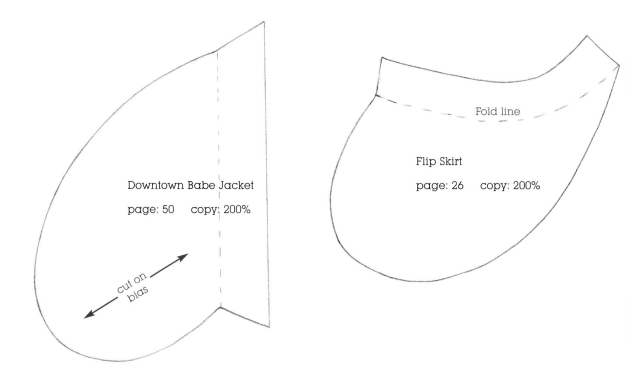

Downtown Babe Jacket

page: 50   copy: 200%

cut on bias

Fold line

Flip Skirt

page: 26   copy: 200%

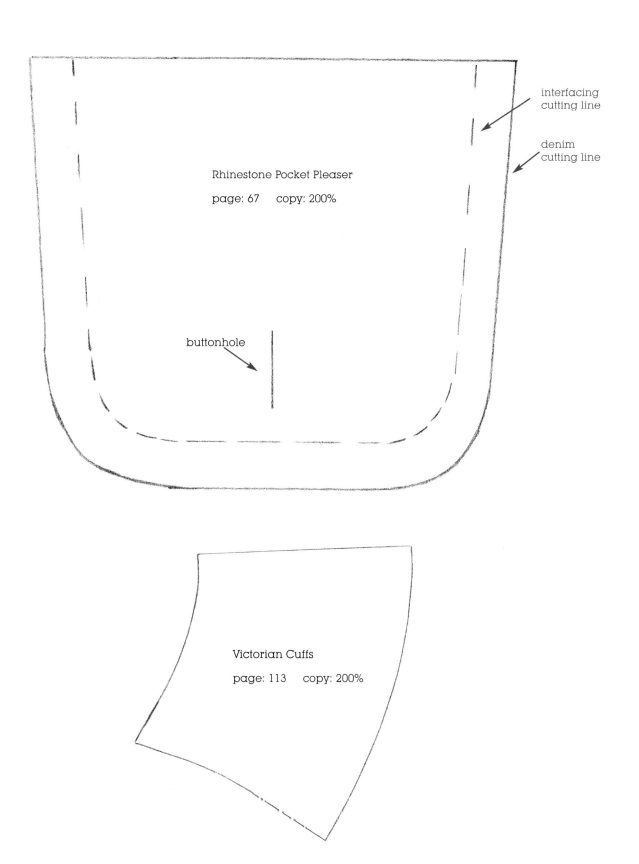

interfacing
cutting line

denim
cutting line

Rhinestone Pocket Pleaser

page: 67   copy: 200%

buttonhole

Victorian Cuffs

page: 113   copy: 200%

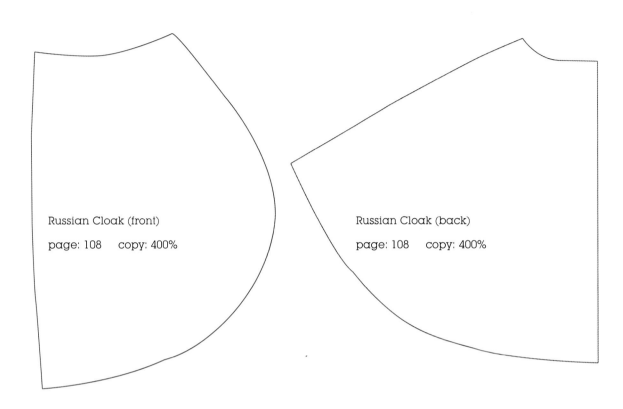

Russian Cloak (front)

page: 108   copy: 400%

Russian Cloak (back)

page: 108   copy: 400%

Pattern Making

Cutting Line

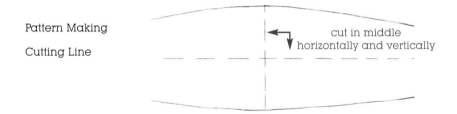

cut in middle
horizontally and vertically

Pattern Making

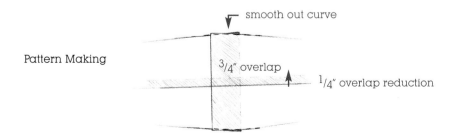

smooth out curve

$3/4$" overlap

$1/4$" overlap reduction

glossary

Au courant up-to-date

Button fly jean fly opening with metal tack button closure

Bespoke made-to-measure clothing

Bon courage good luck

Broderie anglaise literally English embroidery, but designers only use the French-origin term when referring to cotton fabric with small cutout embroidery

Charmeuse a soft, shiny, and lustrous satin-weave silk fabric with a crepe weave on the back

Chez moi my home

Du jour literally, of the day; slang term for the latest trend, something that is ultra trendy

Faux fur synthetic fur

Flat-felted describes an overlapped seam that has been top-stitched so no raw edges are exposed on either the right or wrong side

Gauntlet a dress glove that extends above the wrist. Originally worn in medieval times to protect the hands.

Godet a piece of fabric that is inserted to add fullness

Harlequin a clown dressed in a colorful diamond patchwork

Indigo a deep blue dye obtained from the indigo plant

Pile Fur and some fabrics, like velvet, have long hairs or fibers on the surface and this is called a pile. The pile should always be cut in the same direction because the color changes by how it reflects light. For velvet, it is traditionally cut running up.

Fur is generally cut with the pile running down.

Repeat the repetition of a plaid or print in the cloth

Rivet a metal cap on a fabric's face clamped to a shank that passes through the cloth; used to securely tack denim pocket.

Savoir faire to know the best way to do or say something

Tack button a metal button clamped to a shank slipped through the cloth

Terrible excellent, terrific

Vinyl a synthetic leather fabric

Worsted wool a slick, smooth wool fabric woven with smooth, twisted yarns

special thanks

Thank you Lee Jeans for generously supplying me with samples.

Special thanks to the Models for their enthusiasm:

Gwénäelle Doulie

Nathalie Ermgodts

Doris Claesen by Flag Agency (http://www.flagmodels.com)

Girls by Dominique Models Agency Brussels (http://www.dominique-models.be):

Marine Carton

Isabelle De Meyer

An Hordies

Charlotte Van Cranenbroeck

index